3/6 net
1/9

GEORGE BUCHANAN

GEORGE BUCHANAN.
(*From Boissard.*)

GEORGE BUCHANAN

A BIOGRAPHY

BY

D. MACMILLAN, M.A., D.D.

MINISTER OF KELVINHAUGH PARISH, GLASGOW

AUTHOR OF

"JOHN KNOX, A BIOGRAPHY"

EDINBURGH

GEORGE A. MORTON, 42 GEORGE STREET

LONDON: SIMPKIN, MARSHALL, & CO. LTD.

1906

To

ROBERT FLINT

D.D., LL.D., F.R.S.E.

EMERITUS PROFESSOR OF DIVINITY IN THE UNIVERSITY OF EDINBURGH
CORRESPONDING MEMBER OF THE INSTITUTE OF FRANCE AND
HONORARY MEMBER OF THE ROYAL SOCIETY OF PALERMO

REPRESENTATIVE

IN THE TWENTIETH CENTURY AS

GEORGE BUCHANAN

WAS IN THE SIXTEENTH OF

SCOTTISH LEARNING AND

SCHOLARSHIP

PREFACE

HAD Mr. Robert Wallace, M.P. for East
Edinburgh, lived to finish his biography of
George Buchanan, this work would probably have
never been written. But all that he left was a frag-
ment in the form of "characteristics," rich and
suggestive so far as it goes; the life proper
abruptly stops in its opening chapter. Apart from
that there is no other biography of Buchanan
which attempts to give, within a brief compass,
the story of his chequered and remarkable career.
It accordingly occurred to me that as the countrymen of Buchanan had resolved to commemorate the
quater-century of his birth, which falls this year,
they would not take it amiss if I attempted to write
his Life after the same manner as I did that of his

great contemporary, John Knox, last year. The generous reception given to that work inspired me with a hope that the same favour might be extended to a companion volume. There are, of course, two well-known biographies of Buchanan in existence—the one by Dr. David Irving and the other by Dr. P. Hume Brown. But they are written on a large scale and give what may be termed a scientific, full, and exhaustive representation of their subject. Everyone who is desirous of learning all that can be known of Buchanan must turn to them, especially to Dr. Hume Brown's, to which I owe much, and my effort will not have been in vain if it should direct the attention of readers to its informative and interesting pages. I am further indebted to its author for permission to publish his translations of certain of Buchanan's verses. It would be impossible, as it may be unnecessary, to refer in detail to my other sources of obligation. The literature on the period, if not on the subject, is almost inexhaustible.

I have again to express my thanks to Mr. William Wallace, LL.D., for valuable suggestions made

while the work was passing through the press ; to the
Rev. George Drummond, B.D., for kindly revising
the proofs; and to the Rev. R. S. V. Logie, M.A., for
preparing the Index. I am also under very special
obligation to the Librarian of Glasgow University
and his assistants for putting the resources of their
Library so generously at my service.

D. M.

March 1906.

CONTENTS

LIST OF ILLUSTRATIONS

xiii

GEORGE BUCHANAN

———+———

CHAPTER I

THE SCHOLAR

THERE is not the same uncertainty regarding the early years of George Buchanan as there is about those of his great fellow-countryman and contemporary, John Knox. The reformer's *History of the Reformation of Religion in Scotland* gives full and graphic details of the writer's life during its latest period, but about its opening years it maintains a singular silence. Buchanan in his old age, in response, it is believed, to the entreaties of his friends, wrote a brief record of his life, and his narrative has formed the basis of every biography of him that has since appeared. It stops short at his final arrival in Scotland in 1561, but his career from that date till his death can be traced from other sources, and thus a full sketch of his life is possible. Nor is there any doubt as to the date of his birth. He himself tells us that he was born about the beginning of February 1506.

The village of Killearn, in Stirlingshire, claims the honour of being Buchanan's birthplace, but it was two miles beyond it, near the river Blane, on the lands of Moss or Mid-Leowen, that he was born. Nothing now remains of the house; but a table and a chair, made from one of the oaken rafters, are still shown in the more modern structure which has taken its place. The question of heredity, which plays so important a part in modern biographical writing, is of special significance in relation to the life and character of Buchanan. He is recognised on all hands to have been a typical Scot, and to have, more than most, possessed the *præfervidum ingenium Scotorum*, which he himself was the first to declare to be characteristic of his countrymen. He was of mixed descent. His father was a Celt and his mother was a Teuton. This combination, in its purity, of the two chief elements which compose the Scottish nation, accounts in the eyes of some for the rare genius of Buchanan. In any case, it merits attention, even although no large generalisation can be drawn from it.

The Buchanans from whom he was descended trace their origin from the eleventh century. Their genealogical tree in its earliest branches is probably mythical. The clan claims as its ancestor one Anselan Okyan, a fugitive from Ireland, who sought safety in Scotland from the vengeance that pursued him on account of the part which he had taken in a general slaughter of the Danes. Landing on the west coast, he settled in Lennox, and his family, by royal favour and prudent marriages, became considerable landowners in the district, and possessors of Buchanan. After a time they assumed the territorial name, but their original designation is held to be still found in the Macauslans and Macmillans, who are equally entitled to the benefactions and Scholarships of the clan, of which they are branches. Critics of Buchanan's life have not failed to point to the fact of his connection with the house of Lennox. Through the Drumikill branch of the family to which he belonged, he was directly descended from Murdach, Duke of Albany, and Isobel, heiress of Lennox. His blood connection with Darnley, the husband of Queen Mary, thus accounts to some for the side that he took in the rebellion that banished Mary to England, and set her son on the throne. We can hardly conceive, however, that a man of Buchanan's culture and power of detachment would be thus prejudiced in judging of so great a cause. But even Knox was not impervious to that feudal relationship which was of so great influence during the long period of the Middle Ages, and from which the country was only emerging. His comparatively gentle treatment of Bothwell is thus explained, for Knox himself tells the earl that his ancestors had served his lordship's family in battle. But of one thing there can be no doubt: Buchanan's sympathy for the Celtic element in the Scottish nation reveals itself in his writings, particularly in his " History." Gaelic was his mother-tongue. His father was a Highlander, and in recounting the valour of the Scottish nation, it was the race from which he was descended that he had in mind. However much of the lowland Scot can be seen in his temperament, his love for and admiration of the race from which he sprang, unconsciously coloured his *Rerum Scoticarum Historia*, his longest and most ambitious work.

His mother was a native of East Lothian. Her name was Agnes Heriot, and her family had for many generations been possessors of the lands of Trabroun, near Lauder. George Heriot, the founder of Heriot's Hospital, claimed connection with the same family. He also, like his more distinguished relative, had intimate dealings with King James the Sixth, and the monarch no doubt would find them more agreeable than those he had with Buchanan. A prince like James would be sure to appreciate the liberality of his banker more than the strictness of his tutor. Circumstances soon arose which tested to the utmost the character of Agnes Heriot. Her husband died before he had reached middle life, and left her to struggle as best she could with a young family of five sons and three daughters. The grandfather, Robert Buchanan, was still alive, but he was practically insolvent, and the mother was compelled to leave the paternal home and find the means of supporting her children elsewhere. In 1513, when George was seven years old, the lease of certain lands near Cardross, Menteith, was granted to her, and to her sons, Patrick, Alexander, and George. As this lease was renewed in 1531, it would seem that she passed the remainder of her days in the district. In any case, she was able by her thrift and good management to rear her family, all of whom reached maturity, and if one can judge from the future careers of two of her sons, Patrick and George, she was also able to give them a good education. Patrick, like his more distinguished brother, became a scholar, and accompanied him in his scholastic adventure to Portugal; but he died early.

No authentic record remains of the school or schools in which Buchanan received his education. He himself says in his autobiography that he was educated in the "schools of his native country," and it has been inferred that Killearn or Dumbarton, or both, must be referred to. There were good schools in both places, particularly at Dumbarton, and it has been concluded, from the familiar manner in which he writes in his "History" about its castle, that he was educated there. Elementary and Secondary education in Scotland were much more widely spread and advanced before the Reformation than is generally supposed. The

Reformers are credited with being the founders of Scottish education. This is not the case: it was the Roman Church that established the schools and Universities of Scotland, and it was only after it found that the intellectual weapons which it furnished were being turned against itself, that it endeavoured to stem the tide of learning. The Reformers certainly battled against this spirit of reaction, and, valuing at its true price what enlightenment had done for religion, strove to place the education of the country, from its lowest to its highest stage, on a sound basis.

Indeed, generations before Buchanan was born, schools, singularly well equipped, were to be found in many parts of Scotland. They were originally attached to the cathedrals, abbeys, and collegiate churches; but Grammar Schools soon sprang up in the more important towns and burghs, and town councils began to vie with the ecclesiastical authorities in their interest in education. The control of these schools, to begin with, was in the hands of the Church, but its right of management, in certain cases, was contested; the burghs maintaining that it was in their hands the appointment of the master should rest. Such disputes, which were not infrequent, show the lively concern that was taken in education by the citizens, and account, among other things, for the remarkable part which the people, as a whole, took in the Reformation of Religion which soon followed: the schools which were founded for the purpose of training young lads for the priesthood having grown into seminaries for the education of Scottish youth. The character of the instruction given will surprise those who, ignorant of our history, imagine that it is in our own time only the country has risen to its true needs in education.

To take one instance among many. From the statutes of the Grammar School of Aberdeen, which are dated prior to the Reformation, and refer to a period earlier still, in all probability to the beginning of the sixteenth century, the very time when Buchanan would be at school, we learn that the boys had to acquire a moderate knowledge of arithmetic, and that the "master prelected on Terence, Virgil, or Cicero, and that the boys were strictly forbidden to speak in the vulgar tongue, but only in Latin, Greek, Hebrew, French, and Gaelic." Granting that this course did not prevail

in all the other schools in the country, it at any rate
gives a fair indication of the kind of instruction
imparted to certain of the Scottish youth before
the Reformation. In the light of it, the famous
Act of 1496, which ordains that "all burghesses and
freeholders of substance shall send their eldest sons
and heirs to school, from they be eight or nine
years of age; and to remain there until they be
competently grounded and have perfect Latin,"
was evidently no dead letter. Even though the
instruction given was not of so thorough a character
as could be desired, no boy of ordinary intelligence
could have passed through such a course of study
without receiving a very considerable amount of
culture.

Of one thing we may be certain : young Buchanan
would take full advantage of every opportunity
for mental training which the schools of his native
country afforded him. Indeed, this is put beyond
doubt by the fact that his uncle, his mother's
brother, James Heriot, struck by the ability and
industry of the boy, determined to send him to
the University of Paris. This famous seat of
learning had during the Middle Ages stepped into

the first place, and was, at the opening of the sixteenth century, the centre around which the learning and culture of Europe gathered. Buchanan could of course have gone to one or other of the Scottish Universities, three of which, St. Andrews, Glasgow, and Aberdeen, had by this time been founded; but they were meagrely endowed and poorly equipped, and any youth who was looking forward to the career of a scholar was bound to regard the University of Paris as the Alma Mater that would nurture him into position and fame. Buchanan was only fourteen years of age when he left his native land, and began that wandering life which was to be his fate until he had almost approached old age. Whether his early environment influenced him much or not, we cannot tell, but there was no district in Scotland that could be more favourable to the muse than the "varied realms of fair Menteith." But the scenery which inspired his great successor, Sir Walter Scott, would seem to have made no impression on him. Three centuries had to elapse before the *Lady of the Lake* could be written, and the Trossachs receive that meed of praise which was their due.

CHAPTER II

IT must have been a strange experience for a young Scotch lad of fourteen, to find himself suddenly transported from the wild moors of his native country to the seething population and complex civilisation of a cosmopolitan city like Paris. The journey, even, must have been a trying and dangerous ordeal, for the seas were infested with pirates, and the small craft which in those days were the means of communication with the Continent, stood in no little danger of shipwreck. It is more than likely that Buchanan had as companions on the journey fellow-students who also looked to Paris for that mental equipment which they could not find in their own country. Indeed, ever since the founding of the Scots College in 1325, the University of Paris was regarded by the Scottish

youth as an intellectual shrine, towards which they
repaired in ever-growing numbers. Recent research
makes it almost certain that at the time of
Buchanan's first visit to Paris there would at least be
two hundred Scotch lads studying at its University.
The young student's loneliness would accordingly
not be so pronounced as might at first sight appear.
Besides, there had been for many centuries the closest
relations between the two countries, and a Scottish
youth on landing at a French seaport would feel
himself to be no stranger.

The mediæval Universities, especially the large
ones like that of Paris, gathered round them aspiring
youths from every country on the continent of
Europe. Among the ten thousand students who
attended the fifty colleges that formed this famous
University, there would be found a spirit of cosmo-
politanism which would at once put a stranger at
his ease, and unconsciously produce that very culture
which it is the aim of the highest education to
promote. In this lies the significance of a University which has for its first object the removal
of prejudices, national as well as personal, and the
development in the breasts of the students of a

reverence for that humanity which is common to all.

The University of Paris was beginning at this time to lose the high position which it had held for centuries. Its history, from its earliest beginnings in the Middle Ages, had been one of steady growth and of brilliant achievements. For many centuries it was the centre of light and leading for the whole of Europe, and the greatest scholars of every Christian nation either studied or taught in it; but at the time of Buchanan's arrival it was brought face to face with the two great movements which have revolutionised modern Europe: the New Learning and the New Religion. Unfortunately for itself the University of Paris opposed both movements, and the loss of its ancient position and prestige was only a matter of time.

It may be useful to trace, in a word, the course of learning in Europe from the fall of the Roman Empire to the Reformation. With the breaking up of the power of the Cæsars, there was a wild rush of the barbaric hordes over Italy, quickly followed by the corruption of the Latin language and the destruction of the Classical literature and learning. The Church, however, found it necessary, for its own salvation, to preserve at least a semblance of knowledge, for it could not exist without its liturgies, manuals, canon law, and the Scriptures. The preservation of Latin within the Church was thus a necessity, but it became greatly corrupted, and even in its debased form could only be read by the better educated of the clergy. Classical Latin very soon was altogether unknown. The Church also established schools, colleges, and universities for the education of its priesthood, but their purpose being thus confined, education, in the highest sense of the word, could be but very rarely attained.

The philosophy which sprang up was naturally influenced by the spirit of the times, which again was but the expression of the policy of the Church. During the long course of centuries a great body of doctrine had been put together, and the questions which began to trouble men's minds were: Is this doctrine true? Does it approve itself to reason? Has it a basis in fact, and does it correspond to what is actual and real in the world and in the life of man? To answer these questions was the great task of the Scholastic philosophy. The most acute minds of the Middle Ages got to be absorbed in them, and the Church felt that its very existence depended on their being answered in the affirmative. This philosophy, at its inception, was a genuine product of the age, and for many centuries it afforded scope for the exercise of the finest talent, but after a time it became unreal; its foundations were shaken, men's minds had outgrown it, and the endless quibbles and inanities into which it had degenerated in the hands of the later Schoolmen, brought it into universal contempt.

From the dying embers of the old philosophy a new flame of light was beginning to shine. The very men who might be expected to hand on the torch of Scholasticism were soon to find more congenial exercise for their talent in the literature of Greece and Rome, which had again been discovered, and was being brought into the full light of day. The breaking up of the Byzantine Empire drove into Italy a number of learned Greeks, who brought with them the literary treasures of their own country. The new learning, as it was called, speedily found many admirers : a fresh world was opened up, and scholarly minds turned away with something like contempt from the old and fruitless studies to a perusal of the immortal literary productions of the Ancient world. In them they discovered those eternal truths which are common to humanity, expressed in the most perfect form and clothed in the choicest language. A revolution took place in men's mental outlook, and a general discarding of Scholasticism could only be a matter of time.

Following quickly upon this intellectual movement came the religious. The failure of the Scholastic philosophy to prove the reality of the doctrines of the Roman Church ended in a scepticism which, if not altogether hostile to religion, welcomed secular studies, which seemed to embody the emancipation of the human spirit ; and it only required the vigorous onslaught of Luther on the old Faith, to usher in the Reformation. The attention of the world began at the same time to be directed to the corruptions and abuses of the Church. The immoral lives of the clergy were a scandal which the consciences of men found it harder every day to tolerate. Their ignorance, too, was colossal, and a combination of circumstances thus arose which called for a speedy and radical reformation of religion.

It might be thought that a lead to these two movements would be given by the Universities, and particularly by the greatest and most famous of them all, that of Paris. But ancient institutions do not readily yield to reform, much less lead it. They have vested interests which they jealously guard; and changes in their constitution usually come from without, and seldom from within their walls. The University of Paris steadily and bitterly opposed these two movements, and the battle was reaching its height at the time when Buchanan arrived in France. The conflict which was being waged must have startled his youthful spirit. His own country, when he left it, was to all appearances enveloped in the clouds and mists of the Middle Ages. Patrick Hamilton had not yet returned from the Continent to preach the doctrines of Luther. Some years had still to elapse before the smoke from the protomartyr's funeral

2

pyre would infect as many as it blew upon. Neither had Sir David Lyndsay written any of his satires against the Church and clergy. The schools and Universities of the country were still in the bonds of Scholasticism. The breath of the new learning had, except perhaps by Gavin Douglas, who translated the *Æneid* into the vernacular, been inhaled by no one.

Young Buchanan, so far, must have been a genuine product of the Middle Ages, and the two years passed by him in the University of Paris would be full of spiritual and mental excitement. Without a minute's warning he was thrown from an old world into a new. We shall see how he profited by this experience. He faced the problems of his new environment and age with an open and candid mind, frankly accepted the new learning, and, after careful and patient investigation, the doctrines of the new religion as well. In a truer sense than either Erasmus or Luther, he was both Humanist and Reformer. Erasmus never left the Roman Church, and Luther always made literature subservient to religion; but Buchanan, who in his early days, and during the greater part of his life,

was a votary of Humanism, nevertheless signalised
his advent as a poet by satirising the clergy, and
ended his career as a member and Moderator of
the Reformed Church of Scotland.

The University of Paris missed its chance. As
the advocates of classical studies were, as a rule,
the men who called for a reform of religion, those
in authority looked upon the two movements as
one, and endeavoured to their very utmost to put
both down. They succeeded, possibly beyond their
expectations, and certainly above their deserts.
For a time, under the patronage of Francis the
First and his famous sister Margaret of Navarre,
the two movements made considerable progress;
but the theologians, feeling convinced that if they
yielded, their old position and influence would be
gone, took advantage of the captivity of the king
in 1525, to drive from the country Lefèvre
d'Étaples, the most liberal minded and advanced
man in the University, and the leader of the
Humanistic movement. Again in 1534, when the
followers of Luther, by a rash movement, put
themselves in the wrong, Francis, believing that
his interests lay with the old party, withdrew his

countenance from the advocates of reform. The
University feeling its position thus strengthened
and backed up by the Parliament and king, practically sealed its fate as the centre of European
culture. Its decay was gradual, however, and
during the time of Buchanan's connection with it
as a Student and Regent, it held its place, but
with steadily diminishing prestige and glory.

There is some difficulty in describing the studies
which were pursued by students attending the
Universities of the Middle Ages, for the course
followed at one period was not the same as at
another. Generally speaking, the student who was
looking forward to the degree of Bachelor was
supposed to apply himself to Logic, but we learn
from Buchanan that the composition of Latin
verse was his chief occupation during his first two
years residence in Paris. "Partly of his own
choice," he says, "and partly of compulsion, the
writing of Latin verse, then the one subject prescribed for boys, made the chief part of his literary
studies." For the degree of Bachelor, which could
not be taken before the age of fourteen, two years
of study were necessary, after which the student

took up the subjects for the degree of Master, which might be conferred on him at twenty-one. He was at liberty then to make choice of Law, Medicine, or Theology, and if successful he received the degree of Doctor at thirty-five. Students of all ages were to be found at the University of Paris, for it embraced the whole sphere of education. It was a school as well as a college. Boys were taught the rudiments of Latin, and even reading and writing. They then might pass on through the different stages to the highest subjects taught.

Most of the students attending the University resided in lodgings, and only a very limited number boarded in the colleges or in the Pedagogia attached to them. Buchanan gives us no information as to where or how he lived, but as he was not a Bursar, and his means were very limited, it is more than likely that he lodged in the town. The life of many of the students, when not engaged at their respective colleges, would seem to have been of an easy, if not of a rough and boisterous nature. They had many privileges, of which they took full advantage, and seized others to which they had no right. At times, especially on the occasion of some great fête, they acted with violence, and became a terror and a danger to the citizens. It can readily be conceived what lawless power could be exercised by the thousands of young men who attended the University when they combined for any particular purpose. They maltreated, robbed, and even assassinated the lieges, and the civil authorities felt compelled to pass laws for the purpose of restraining their conduct and punishing them. But they continued to defy all authority, and to break out periodically into violence. Other times other manners, still the spirit of youth, as seen in the modern student, is not very dissimilar from that displayed in earlier ages. It may express itself in ways less reprehensible, but it seems to be incapable of repression.

Buchanan took full advantage of his opportunities at Paris. He then laid the foundation of his great scholarship, and became an adept in writing Latin verse, an accomplishment which was the great ambition of most scholars at the time. He might have gained more advantage from his dexterity in this art if he had applied his knowledge of easy and correct expression to writing his native

tongue. But his choice was inspired by the custom
of his age, which found in Latin the only language
common to learned men, and by the belief that in
it the literature of the future would be written.
Had Buchanan known that in another hundred
years Latin would be practically discarded, and that
the nations of Western Europe would vie with
each other in bringing to perfection their mother-
tongue, he might have paid less attention to it
and more to the language which Knox was about
to handle with striking effect, and which was soon
to be the vehicle for a literature that the world
will not readily let die. Buchanan was a poet,
and a master of style in prose and verse, and the
Revolution that his country was about to pass
through would have given the inspiration. If he
had but written in the vernacular, and expended
the same pains on his compositions as on his Latin
works, he would have left not only a great name
behind him, but productions which would have
influenced the literary history of the nation, and
been a source of pleasure to his countrymen even
still.

Two events happened at this time which put an

end to Buchanan's studies at the University of
Paris: the death of his uncle and his own illness.
Poverty and disease are bad enough separately, but
they form a combination to which even the strongest
must yield. They were seldom absent from
Buchanan's life. He was in truth a poor scholar
to the end, and his straitened circumstances must
have affected his health, which was never very strong.
He was often in want and often at the point of
death. Nothing, accordingly, remained for him at
this time but to return to Scotland.

CHAPTER III

THE SOLDIER

A YEAR'S rest at his home in Cardross, Menteith,
would seem to have restored Buchanan to
health, at all events he felt himself strong enough to
join in a warlike expedition against England. His
native country was at this time under a regency, King
James the Fifth being a minor. After the death of
James the Fourth, on the fatal field of Flodden, the
Government fell into the hands of the Queen-Mother,
who was a sister of Henry the Eighth. On her marriage with the Earl of Angus, the nobles, jealous of the
power thus placed in the hands of one of their own
order, recalled the Duke of Albany, High Admiral of
France and cousin of the late King, to his native
country, and made him Regent. This kindled afresh
the fears of Henry the Eighth, who saw in the
appointment a menace on the part of France, and

in order to weaken, or if possible to break up the alliance between the two countries, always regarded as the enemies of England, he sent a force across the border.   Albany met this force, and came to an understanding with its leaders.   He then returned to France ; but, on hearing that a large English army had again invaded Scotland, he returned with a band of auxiliaries in the autumn of 1523, and after resting at Glasgow marched to the Boroughmuir, near Edinburgh, where he was joined by a large body of Scottish nobles and men-at-arms.

On the first blush it may seem strange that a young man like Buchanan, now in his eighteenth year, of delicate constitution and scholarly habits, should venture on so dangerous and trying an expedition.   But the love of battle was in his blood.   He had inherited it from his ancestors. The passages in his " History " which relate to warlike encounters, are written in the style of one who knew and sympathised with the soldier's calling.   Indeed, he seemed to share Carlyle's belief, that the great man is capable of any work or enterprise, and that his occupation is pretty much a matter of accident. In any case, he saw nothing incongruous in the

professional man of letters acting the soldier. In
the dedication of his *Jephthes* to the Maréchal de
Brissac, he says: "There is no discord, as is
commonly but erroneously supposed, between the
study of the art of war and of letters, but rather
the greatest concord, and a certain secret and natural
congruity. For all great commanders, in all ages,
who have performed illustrious actions, have either
been themselves very learned men, or have cherished,
with the greatest affection, men distinguished for
learning." Buchanan's ambition, we know, was to
be a great scholar, he may have been desirous of
becoming a great soldier as well; at all events, he
tells us that his object in joining the expedition
was to learn the military art. He never had
occasion afterwards to practise it as a soldier, but
it must have stood him in good stead in describing
the battles with which his " History " abounds.

Albany marched south as far as Melrose, intending to cross to the English side by a bridge which
spanned the Tweed there; but the Scots, who saw
in the expedition an attempt on the part of France
to checkmate England, quite as much as an honest
endeavour to protect Scotland, declined to cross

the border. Indeed, it was suspected that if
Scotland would drop the French alliance, English
invasions would be few and far between. Albany
then marched south until he came opposite to
Wark Castle, which he determined to take. This
he found a task beyond his power. The French
auxiliaries besieged it with very barren results. The
Regent determined to retreat, and in his march,
near Lauder, his army was overtaken by a severe
snowstorm, which impeded his progress and lost him
many men. The English also disbanded their forces
and returned home. Buchanan survived the expedition, but returned in shattered health to Cardross,
where he was bedfast for the rest of the winter.

Buchanan did not remain long enough at the
University of Paris to entitle him to the degree of
Bachelor. Accordingly, in the following spring he
matriculated, along with his eldest brother Patrick,
at the University of St. Andrews. As he was
granted his certificate the following year, the period
during which he studied at Paris must have counted.
This was according to the regulations which governed
the mediæval Universities. All of them being under
the Church, they were affiliated to each other, and

recognised each other's degrees. A distinction, after a time, was made by the University of Paris, which naturally had some hesitation in recognising the hall-mark of some of the younger and small schools of learning. This brotherhood was of great service in spreading culture, for a graduate of one University could go to another, and begin teaching at once as Regent. This to a certain extent explains the frequent and close intercommunion that existed between the Universities of mediæval Europe. The travelling scholar was as much a sign of the learned life of those days, as the resident professor or tutor is of ours.

The University of St. Andrews had on its teaching staff at this time one man of marked distinction, the renowned schoolman, John Major. He had studied at Cambridge and Oxford, had received his doctorate from Paris, and was then and afterwards held in the highest regard as the leading exponent of Scholasticism. Major, who was a man of un-doubted talents and of great learning, was unfortun-ate in the hour of his birth. He stood at the meeting of the waters. The old and the new in literature and religion were beginning to come into

collision at the very time when he entered on his
life's work. He cannot be said to have been the
offspring of both movements. His mind was
moulded by the Scholastic philosophy, and in spite
of certain ideas which he held regarding the
relations between a prince and his subjects, he was
a strenuous upholder of use and wont in Church
and State. A native of North Berwick, he is
believed by some to have received his early education at the Grammar School of Haddington, which
Knox must have also attended, but, like the other
scholars of the time, he found his way to Paris, and
became identified with the Collége Montaigu, the
most reactionary in the University. He acquired,
while teaching there, a great reputation as an
exponent, after the accepted method, of the
Aristotelian logic, but he is now chiefly remembered
for his *History of Britain*, which is full of interesting
details, passed over by a writer like Buchanan, who
took a broad view of his subject. His style has
been severely criticised for its lack of literary grace
and finish, but the book gives proof of a strong
talent, which accounts in some measure for the high
position awarded to its author by his contemporaries.

Major returned to his native country in 1518, and for the next seven years he acted as Regent in the Universities of Glasgow and St. Andrews. He must have found a vast difference between his new surroundings and those to which he had been accustomed in Paris. Even the oldest and richest of the Scottish Universities, that of St. Andrews, was miserably poor in buildings, endowments, and teaching equipment. The fame and ability of Major would no doubt put some heart and life into them; but even half a century later, the University of Glasgow was in so disorganised and hopeless a condition, that it was only saved from threatened extinction by the genius and labours of Andrew Melville. The higher education in Scotland has had to struggle against the dire odds of poverty, yet it is one of the chief glories of the nation, that in spite of every difficulty it has held its own as one of the best-educated countries in the world.

Major, it has been remarked, on his return to Scotland, acted for some time as one of the Regents in St. Andrews University. This was a post common to all the mediæval Universities, and as reference to it frequently occurs in the life of

Buchanan, it may be necessary to define both it and
the other terms applied to the various offices and
duties of the staff in pre-Reformation Universities.
These terms still linger on, although they have lost
their original meaning.

The Scottish Universities were founded on the
model of those of the Continent, particularly on two,
the Universities of Bologna and Paris. Each had
at its head a Chancellor, who represented the
authority of the Church, and guarded the rights of
the University as an ecclesiastical rather than a
civil institution. It also had its Rector, who was
elected by the students, and who protected their
privileges against the encroachments of both Church
and State. His electors were the four Nations into
which the University was divided, and this custom
still holds good in the Universities of Glasgow and
Aberdeen. This division into Nations was geo-
graphical, and served a double purpose. Students
found on their arrival at any centre of learning an
incorporation, akin to them by blood and traditions,
which gave them a ready welcome, and the home
students were at the same time prevented from
having the sole management in University life and

affairs. The men who managed the election of the Rector were the Procurators, who acted as the heads of the nations. The Censor was the officer who kept a watchful eye on the conduct of the students, both in the college and in the streets. The brains of the University were the Regents, who composed the teaching staff. On their ability and learning, the success of the Institution mainly depended. The power to lecture was not then in the hands of a close corporation. Every student on graduating was entitled to teach in any University, and from among them a body were selected, termed Regents, to whom certain powers of government were entrusted. The Doyen has his modern representative in the Deacon or Dean who is the head of his faculty, whether it be that of Divinity, Medicine, or Law. The Bursarius is perhaps the most living of all, for, owing to the multiplication of endowments, chiefly in the form of scholarships, the bursar is much in evidence among the students of the Scottish Universities.

Major, while at St. Andrews, lectured on logic, and apparently to the dissatisfaction of Buchanan. The subject in itself is sufficiently interesting, and very

3

helpful for mental training. But in the hands of the Schoolmen it had become worse than useless, for their endless hairsplitting and learned trifling filled the youthful and ingenuous mind with a feeling of contempt and disgust. Buchanan has left on record his opinion of Major's teaching: " It was the art of Sophistry rather than dialectics "; in other words, it was so much wind. A mind like Buchanan's longed for realities; all that Major could offer was inanities. The learned doctor of the Sorbonne came afterwards under the lash of Melanchthon and Rabelais. A new spirit had dawned which he could not comprehend. This was his misfortune rather than his fault.

Buchanan finished his course on the 3rd of October 1525, when he took the degree of Bachelor. He availed himself of his circumstances to escape the fees for the degree. This was a common custom at all the Universities, and the term pauper applied to such did not convey the idea of unmerited reproach which it now bears. It simply meant that the student's condition entitled him to a certain exemption, of which he could take advantage without any dishonour.

Buchanan had by this time made choice of his

future career: he determined to be a scholar; and, as a degree from the University of Paris would be of the greatest service to him, he was fortunate in receiving a nomination as Bursar in the Scots College there. It is supposed by some that he owed this favour to his old teacher, John Major. This opinion is grounded on a sentence in Buchanan's autobiography, in which he states that he followed Major to Paris. But there was evidently very little sympathy between the two men, and Buchanan, having taken only a second class for the degree of Bachelor, could have had no claim on Major's generosity. It is as well to make this clear, for the manner in which Buchanan afterwards spoke of his old teacher is a proof to some of that spirit of ingratitude, vindictiveness, and badness of heart with which he is charged. Buchanan, from his connection with the Lennox family, could not have been without sufficient influence to gain him entrance as Bursar into the Scots College. The fact of his following Major at the interval of half a year is surely very slender ground for the assertion that it was to the old doctor of the Sorbonne he owed this favour. Major has come down to posterity pilloried by

Buchanan in an epigram which is as severe and stinging as anything he ever wrote. It must be confessed that, if the writer had been indebted to the subject of his satire, his verse would be quite unpardonable. Major, playing on his own name, and secure in the position which he occupied in the learned world, had spoken of himself as *Joannes solo cognomine Major* (Major by name and not by nature). Taking this as his text, Buchanan wrote the following merciless epigram :

> "'Major by name,' thou sayst, 'and not by nature,'
>   The greatest liars sometimes speak the truth,
> And in thy endless stream of idle chatter
>   What wonder if thou once hast spoken sooth."

Buchanan, by the time he had written this, had openly identified himself with the Humanistic movement, and had also become affected by the spirit of the Reformation, for he remarks that after his arrival in France at this time he " became tinged with the flame of Lutheranism spreading everywhere." On the two grounds, then, of the new religion and the new learning, he was in deadly opposition to Major and the Schoolmen, and felt warranted, as Erasmus also did, in hurling the

shafts of his satire against them. Opponents spoke
and wrote of each other in those days in a way
which makes the modern man look aghast. It was
the manner of the times, and does not seem to have
given inordinate offence. Otherwise, we can hardly
conceive how Buchanan himself escaped the retribu-
tion which he undoubtedly provoked, but men of
genius have in an age of enlightenment and progress
always manifested keen resentment towards dullards
and obscurantists. Major was probably neither the
one nor the other, but he had been brought up in
the old ways, and had now arrived at a time of life
when it was not easy to leave them. Buchanan, in
satirising the individual, was in fact destroying the
cause which he championed, and thus proving himself
to be a leader of that movement which was revolutionising thought and heralding in a new age.

CHAPTER IV

THE Scots College which Buchanan now entered
had been founded in 1326 by the then Bishop
of Moray. It was small and poor compared with some
of the other Colleges, but it was a welcome haven
for Scotsmen, especially prior to the founding of
their own University of St. Andrews. Buchanan
was now Bachelor, and it was his aim to secure the
degree of Master at the earliest possible moment,
for he would then be entitled to act as Regent in
one of the Colleges, and so be able to support
himself. His position as Bursar procured him his
board and education, but that was all, and how he was
able to provide himself with the other necessaries of
life it is impossible now to say. These, in Buchanan's
case, as in those of the other poor students of the
University, would be few in number, but there is no

record that he was compelled to beg for them, as was not uncommon. We can well believe him, however, when he declares that during these two years he had a "hard struggle with untoward fortune." We are familiar with the hardships of student life in German, and particularly in Scotch, Universities. These, owing to the generosity of multi-millionaires, will probably be things of the past; but the most affecting picture that has been drawn of them must pale before the trials of cold and hunger and severe discipline which were the lot of Buchanan and many of the students of his time.

Two meals a day, for instance, were supposed to be sufficient for the mediæval student: breakfast at ten and supper at five. Only lads of tender years and constitution had extra collations. The staple fare was bread and porridge, with meat and wine on Sundays and holidays. From six in the morning till breakfast, was the chief time for lectures and study. The afternoon was occupied much in the same way, but the evening was generally free for amusements and pleasure. A student's pastime in those days would seem to have been strolling the streets, drinking in taverns, or engaging in those

party fights which often resulted in serious trouble
and bloodshed. The spirit of feudalism still survived, and jousts, tournaments, and the practice of
the military art were regarded as the main forms of
recreation. Participation in these was necessarily
confined to the wealthy. Poorer students had to
seek for less expensive if also less ennobling pleasures.
The hardship of the student's lot, especially during
the winter season, must have been severe in the
extreme. There was no fire in their Colleges or in
their rooms, they had no benches on which to sit,
and they were compelled to lie or recline on the
floor, which was littered with straw. The sanitary
arrangements were of a very primitive order.
Flogging, especially in the Grammar Schools, and
during the first or preparatory years of University
education, was freely indulged in. Only the robust
student could come through such terrible experiences
unscathed. Buchanan was of a delicate constitution,
and we can well believe him when he characterises
his student life in Paris as years of untoward
hardship.

There was a pressing necessity that Buchanan
should take his degree at the earliest moment.

He accordingly graduated as Master in March 1528, and was thus eligible for the position of Regent in the University. He would not seem to have gone long without an appointment, for we find him the following year on the teaching staff of Ste. Barbe, one of the most enlightened and advanced Colleges in the University. Ste. Barbe was of recent origin, but during the some sixty years of its existence it had outstripped all the others in reputation and fame. Its birth was prophetic of its future eminence, for it was the product of a struggle between the popularity of its original founders and the obscurantists, who would restrain their progressive and reforming zeal. Its creators were Geoffroi and Jean Lenormant of the Collége de Navarre. Their popularity and success drew so many students around them that the dullards objected to their sluggish peace being disturbed by the crowds of eager youths who were attracted by the teaching of the two brothers. Geoffroi the elder solved the difficulty by taking the bold step of founding a College of his own, and in 1460 Ste. Barbe was started. Its success was immediate, and it speedily took its place as the leading centre of the rising life and thought of Paris. This, to begin with, was undoubtedly due to the enlightenment of its founders, but not a little of the credit must be placed to the distinguished band of teachers whom they gathered round them. They were the most promising if not the ripest scholars in the University, and were filled with an enthusiasm for the new learning and liberal thought which the University, through the Sorbonne, was doing its very best to repress.

Buchanan's appointment as Regent in this College proves two things: it testifies to his scholarship, and shows the side which he had already taken in the great controversy of the age. The young Scotsman who a few years before had left his native glens in search of learning, had already proved himself a master of his art, and at the age of twenty-three had secured a position which opened out to him future eminence in his profession. He had also shown an open and candid mind, and that he preferred truth to emoluments, the progress of knowledge to personal comfort and material reward.

Ste. Barbe had, to begin with, no especial *clientèle*, it drew its students from every class and nationality ;

but it soon attracted a number of Portuguese, who repaired to Paris in increasing numbers, owing to the demands which the new possessions of Portugal were making for priests who should minister in its Colonial charges. There was a special reason why the Portuguese should have favoured Ste. Barbe, for there was in connection with it at this time one of their countrymen, a distinguished educationalist, Jacques de Gouvéa, who had afterwards close relations with Buchanan and considerable influence over his fortunes.

De Gouvéa desired to purchase the College for the king of Portugal, but he had to remain content with renting it. Under him, as Principal, it continued to flourish, and in so liberal an atmosphere Buchanan found encouragement and scope for the exercise of his great talent and rare scholarship. He was also now placed above the fear of want. His emoluments certainly will seem beggarly in comparison to the lordly salaries that have since been showered on his successors in the teaching of the Humanities, even in our own Universities. But his wants were few, and his love of knowledge would enable him to bear up under the trials and hardships of his lot.

As Regent, he was entitled to board and lodging;
any additional salary would largely depend on the
position which his College held and on his own
reputation, for the Regent was entitled to charge
fees, and the greater the number of students attending his prelections the larger would be his income.
We can accordingly understand the rivalry that would
exist between the forty or fifty Colleges that about
this time composed the University of Paris, and also
between the Regents who were on their teaching
staff. The students could choose their own Colleges
and their own Regents, and in this way the most
capable men and the best teachers were brought to
the front. In Scotland this system, except in St.
Andrews at one time, has never really had a fair
trial; it still flourishes in England, and, under a
different system, it also prevails in Germany.
Competition in teaching, like competition in trade
and commerce, is bound to have a healthy influence.
Protection in this sphere, at least, spells stagnation
and death.

Though thus working under the most liberal-
minded of Principals, and surrounded by colleagues
who held the most advanced views in theology,

science, and art, Buchanan's life was sufficiently
difficult and trying. The hardships of the Regent
would not seem to be much behind those of the
student, and in one of his earliest poems he thus
describes them.

After a day of exacting labour the poor teacher
finds himself at liberty to retire to rest. "No
sooner," he remarks, "has he stretched his limbs
than the watchman announces that it is already the
fourth hour. The din of the shrill alarm chases
away dreams and reminds him that his rest is at an
end. Hardly are things again quiet when five o'clock
sounds, and the porter rings his bell calling the
scholars to their task. Then in all the majesty of
cap and gown forth issues the master, the terror of
his charge, in his right hand the scourge, in his left
perchance the works of the great Virgil. He seats
himself, and shouts his orders till he is red in the
face. And now he brings forth the harvest of his
toil. He smoothes away difficulties, he corrects, he
expunges, he changes the text, he brings to light
the spoils he has won by ceaseless study. Meanwhile his scholars, some of them, are sound asleep,
others thinking of everything but their Virgil. One

is absent, but has bribed his neighbour to answer to his name at roll-call. Another has lost his stockings. Another cannot keep his eye off a large hole in his shoe. One shams illness, another is writing letters to his parents. Hence the rod is never idle, sobs never cease, cheeks are never dry. Then the duties of religion make their call on us, then lessons once more, and once more the rod. Hardly an hour is spared for our meal. No sooner is it over than lessons again, and then a hasty supper. Supper past, we continue our labours into the night as if the day's tasks, forsooth, had not been sufficient. Why should I speak of our thousand humiliations? Here, for example, comes the swarm of loafers from the city, till the street echoes with the noise of their pattens. In they scramble to listen as intelligently as so many asses. They grumble that no placards announcing the scheme of lessons have been stuck on the street corners, they are indignant that the *doctrinal* of Alexander is scornfully ignored by the master, and off they run to Montaigu or some other school more to their taste. Parents also grumble that the days pass by, that their sons learn nothing, and meanwhile the fees must be paid."

Buchanan's whole energies, however, were not absorbed in the trying and not unpainful duties of which he has given so graphic a description. He had a soul above the mere drudgery of his work, and introduced certain reforms in the teaching of Latin which made their mark on the educational methods of the times. In 1533 he published a Latin translation of *Linacre's Grammar*, a thing which in itself might not at first appear to be of any special significance, but it was in keeping with his general attitude towards the old system, not only of teaching but also of thought.

The University of Paris, as has been shown, was the most conservative of institutions, and it was not till 1600 that Greek was formally recognised by it as a subject of study. We can accordingly imagine the opposition which Buchanan would meet in trying to raise its teaching, and particularly by this attempt to dethrone from its time-honoured place the Latin Grammar of Alexander of Villa-dei. *The Rudiments of the Latin Language*, by this celebrated author, had been recognised as the standard work for the teaching of Latin Grammar since the middle of the thirteenth century. Classical

scholars felt that the times had outgrown a handbook written in verses " of which each word is meant
to suggest or recall some rule of Syntax." It had,
besides, during the course of centuries become over-
loaded with notes at the hands of various com-
mentators. Its text, however, was regarded as a
kind of Bible, and it was heresy for any one to doubt
its methods, and rank heresy on the part of him
who would venture to displace it. Buchanan took
this bold step, and his translation of *Linacre's
Grammar*, dedicated to the young Earl of Cassillis,
and printed by Robert Estienne at Paris, went
through seven editions before the century was
out.

It was at this time that Buchanan began to launch
those epigrams against the dull upholders of use and
wont in learning and religion, which made him a
powerful force in the movements of the times. The
opposition to his first literary venture was only an
indication of the strong currents that were then dis-
turbing the intellectual life of Paris. About this
very time two men were associated with Buchanan's
own College of Ste. Barbe, who represented these
cross-currents in their full force and conflict. We

mean Calvin and Loyola. Other names more
prominent at the time, though less distinguished
now, indicate the strong intellectual life that was
animating the University, and which, seemingly
triumphant for the time, was in the end doomed to
stagnation, if not to extinction. Such names as
d'Étaples, Briçonnet, and Guillaume Budé were
thoroughly representative of the best scholarship
and the most advanced thinking on the vital subjects
which are of the deepest interest to the human mind
in all ages, and against these we have the name of
Noel Beda, the Syndic of the University, who was the
incarnation of the reactionary and obscurantist
spirit of the times.

Buchanan's was not yet a name to conjure with,
but, determined to take his part in the great controversy that was being waged, he made use of the
only weapon at his command, that of epigram. In
his hands, as we have already seen from his onslaught
on poor John Major, it proved a most formidable
weapon. Hurled at the leaders of Scholasticism, it
rendered valuable service to the cause that he and
his friends had so much at heart. These epigrams
passed from hand to hand and from mouth to mouth,

4

and while wounding his opponents they reacted on
the author in turn, made him many enemies, and
effectually stopped any probable promotion to the
higher posts in the University. But Buchanan was
no place-hunter; he had not that vulpine cunning
which is often the sole talent of the mediocre mind,
and which by chicanery and fawning flattery
often succeeds where outstanding ability fails. But
such success as mean spirits of this kind achieve,
is after all not worth the having. To possess the
integrity of one's soul, as Buchanan did, and to
sacrifice for the sake of truth mere place and power,
is one of the clearest proofs of a noble nature.
Buchanan in the end attained to greater celebrity
and wielded a higher power, but these were of the
mind and spirit. All true influence in the end is
the expression of a character that can rise above
"the world and the things thereof."

The merits of Buchanan received, on the 3rd of
June 1529, what may be regarded as the first official
recognition; he was on that date elected Procurator
of the German Nation. This position was held for
a month, and he was appointed to it four successive
times. In the following year it fell to the Scottish

section of the German Nation to choose a member
who should represent them in the election of a
Rector. They chose Buchanan, that "able man so
learned in Latin and in Greek." It is not at all
unlikely that had he remained longer in Ste. Barbe,
he would have been appointed to the Rectorship
itself, but he left at the end of three years to become
tutor to the young Earl of Cassillis.

As Buchanan's official connection with the University of Paris now came to an end—if we except
the blank of five years in his life when he is supposed
by some to have been on the teaching staff of the
Collége du Cardinal Lemoine—it may be well to
glance at the character of the education given in
mediæval Universities. The first thing that strikes
one is the extreme youth of many of the students.
Buchanan himself was only a lad of fourteen when
he entered the University of Paris. On the other
hand, we are equally struck by the mature and even
old age of some who would seem to have hung on
to the Universities year after year, without ever
taking a degree. A considerable number, accordingly,
would be too young to profit by the instruction, and
an equally large number too old to respond to that

enthusiasm which should characterise the pursuit of literature and learning. Nor were the teachers always competent. The older members of the staff were in many cases indifferent to their work and disinclined to lecture. The burden fell chiefly on the shoulders of the Regents, who, whatever their ability, were for the most part inexperienced young men. They were, besides, dependent to a large extent for their livelihood on the students, whose part they naturally took, and this weakened that discipline which is absolutely necessary for the success of any institution.

The weight also which the Schoolmen attached to the name of Aristotle, and to the compilers of some of their text-books, repressed the spirit of inquiry, and retarded that progress which results from studying facts in place of books, and a few books at the most. That mental attitude towards history and nature which characterises science, had not yet been adopted. It is upon this that modern education is based, and a perception of its method at once reveals the wide gulf that separates Scholasticism from Humanism and from the intellectual life of our day. But in spite of all this it would be unfair to withhold that meed of praise which is due to the mediæval Universities. They were perhaps as faithful to the light that was in them as their representatives in modern times. They held aloft the torch of knowledge, and, if they were not progressive, they at any rate marked time, and prevented the torch being extinguished. Besides, education after all is largely independent of the subjects taught. We may inveigh against the dog-Latin of the Schoolman and the elegant classicism of the Humanist. But mental training is the main thing, and it must be admitted that the men in the Middle Ages who held the highest positions in Church and State, and who had received their education in the Universities, could easily hold their own as diplomatists and ecclesiastics with their modern successors.

If the description which Buchanan has given of the life of a Regent be half, as we believe it to be wholly, true, he must have quitted Ste. Barbe without much regret. He was now in his twenty-eighth year, and the only post available was that of tutor and companion to a young Scottish nobleman. Buchanan was not adapted by character or temperament for the work of a scholastic drudge. He was a poet and a Celt, and was unsuited to run in harness, especially such harness as bound the mediæval teacher to his task. That he was able to submit to it for so many years was a proof of his extreme poverty and of his remarkable power of will. He could have secured preferment if he had cared. The Church was open to him, and there he might have found the learned leisure for which he no doubt longed. He had not as yet declared for Luther, but according to himself he was affected by his spirit. His hatred of and contempt for the monks who used their cowl as a cover and bait for their wickedness, was soon to find pointed expression. The Church, accordingly, he would not enter; so he had to take the post of tutor, in which he certainly would have more freedom, independence, and time for self-culture than he could have secured in any of the offices in the University for which he might be eligible or to which he could aspire. The time had gone by when the fancy picture which a recent writer draws of the career and fortune of the wandering scholars of the Middle Ages could be true. It never proved true in the case of Buchanan; quite the opposite. Even the more fortunate Erasmus never approached it.

The picture describes these scholars " wandering first over Italy and then over Europe; rising by their own efforts from the position of penniless no-bodies; destitute in many, though not in all, cases of birth, breeding, or wealth; marrying beautiful, rich, and well-born damsels; allured from State to State and from city to city by golden bribes; setting out in quest of the buried treasures of learning like knights of adventure; helping to despatch generation after generation of neophytes, often from half-barbarous nations, to spread learning and the appreciation of beauty all over Europe; honoured in their deaths by stately monuments, and rewarded by posterity for no few generations, not merely as good workers in their day and way, but as men of genius and public benefactors." What a travesty this is of the life of Buchanan; the only word that is true of him is the first—he was a " wanderer."

CHAPTER V

IT was while acting as tutor to the young Earl of Cassillis that Buchanan wrote a poem which had a most important influence on his career and fortunes. In it he threw out a challenge to the Roman Church. His effort was a satire on the Franciscans, one of the most powerful religious bodies of the time. The noble house with which Buchanan was now connected had played a prominent part in Scottish History. His pupil's father had been assassinated in 1527, and his uncle, William Kennedy, the Abbot of Crossraguel, became his guardian, and took him to Paris for the completion of his education. On the young Earl's return in 1535, Buchanan accompanied him, and it was while staying with his charge in the country, as he himself tells us in the dedication of his *Franciscanus* to the Earl of Moray, that his first attack on this famous religious Order was written. Young Cassillis was afterwards one of the Commissioners who represented Scotland at the marriage of Queen Mary to the Dauphin in 1558. This in itself is a proof of the position which he occupied in the eyes of the Scottish Parliament. His connection with a man like Buchanan must have had a powerful influence on his life. What part he might have played in the Revolution that was impending, we cannot tell, for he never returned from France. He was one of the three Commissioners who on their way home died at Dieppe, poisoned, as it was believed, by the Guises.

Buchanan, in thus launching his invective against the religious scandals of the times, was but following in the footsteps of even a greater than he, and one who is regarded as his master. There is perhaps little resemblance between the two great Humanists of the sixteenth century, Erasmus and Buchanan, except in their equal mastery of Latin and their common hatred of the monastic Orders. They were essentially different in character and temperament, but they were alike in their love of letters,

their strenuous advocacy of liberal ideas, and their
unceasing attacks on the scandals and abuses of the
Roman Church. It should not be forgotten that
Erasmus was the precursor of Luther, and that
Buchanan anticipated Knox. It may be true that
the Humanists regarded the prevailing religious
corruptions from one standpoint, and the Reformers
from another. It was the intellectual and moral
sense of Erasmus and Buchanan that revolted against
the terrible abuses of the times; whereas it was the
religious sense of Luther and Knox that was affected.
This at once explains the different methods by
which such leading spirits endeavoured to correct
the errors of the times, and to save the world from
threatened ruin. Satire became the weapon of the
Humanist, theology that of the Reformer.

It is significant that the men who attempted to
reform the Church levelled their attacks against
the monastic orders. These religious bodies had in
fact become all powerful; they had invaded the
sanctity of the home, and were spreading a moral
plague over every country in Christendom. It was
against them that Erasmus directed his sharpest
strokes and shot his wittiest arrows. His humour

found its most poignant and playful expression in
describing their ignorance, sottishness, sensuality,
and hypocrisy. They made every attempt to silence
him—by death if necessary—but he managed to
avoid their ruthless clutch, and before his death he
saw in their discomfiture the triumph of the cause
which he had so brilliantly championed. Buchanan
has also the distinction of breaking fresh ground,
so far as Scotland is concerned. He was the first
to make the monks feel that an intellect of the
highest order saw through their sham religiosity,
and meant to give them no quarter. The movement
for reform had no doubt begun at an earlier date,
for Patrick Hamilton had been already burned;
but Buchanan was the first to bring powers of the
first order, trained to their finest finish, to bear
upon the ecclesiastical abuses and monastic corruptions, which up to his time had been allowed to
grow practically undisturbed and unexposed in
Scotland.

He had as his contemporary Sir David Lyndsay,
who wrote in the Scottish vernacular, and who in
his satires, particularly that of the *Three Estates*,
did full justice to his theme. He certainly did not

spare the Church or Churchmen, and the low level
to which the religious life of the country had fallen
can be seen in the enjoyment with which the people,
from the king upon his throne to the very meanest
of his subjects, witnessed Lyndsay's plays, and
laughed uproariously at his humorous sallies at the
expense of cowled monk and veiled nun. What
surprises us, indeed, is Lyndsay's immunity from
punishment. How he escaped imprisonment and
the stake is inexplicable. The king's protection
must have counted for much, but that continued
only for a season. After the death of James the
Fifth he was at the mercy of Cardinal Beaton, but he
was permitted to die peacefully in bed at a ripe
age. It is instructive to contrast with this leniency
the Church's bitter persecution of Buchanan. He
tells us himself that so strong was their hatred of
him, that because of the poems which he wrote at
this time they drove him into exile, and that while
in exile they " persecuted him with the whole
violence of their authority through England, France,
Spain, and Italy." The fact is, they saw in Buchanan
a foeman worthy of their steel. His reputation and
his Latin verse would carry his opinions over the

whole of Europe. They perceived that his satire
was an appeal, not so much to the moral sense of
Scotland as to the intelligence of the civilised
world.

Some have doubted the sincerity of the Humanists
in their attacks on the Roman Church. They are
of the opinion that they chose such subjects because
they found in them the means for exercising their
wit and displaying their Latinity. They accordingly
discover an insincere ring in their verse, which is on
the whole characterised not so much by art as
artificiality. We do not believe that there is any
truth in this, so far as Buchanan is concerned. He
knew perfectly well the risk he was running. That
he should repeat his attack again and again after
the first significant warning, is surely sufficient proof
that his heart was in his task and that his satires
were the outcome of his deepest convictions. One
cannot give them the most cursory reading without
detecting a savage hatred in them, which, whether
it be artistic or not, is certainly intensely real. For
one of them he suffered an exile of twenty-four
years, which was the alternative to the death that
was intended for him. That a man should court

such a fate because of his vanity in proving that he could write pretty Latin stanzas, passes ordinary belief.

If ever an age lent itself to satire it was that of Erasmus and Buchanan. It found its parallel in that of Lucian, when the "gods were dethroned from Olympus, and no new ones had been put in their place." The moral corruptions of the time were the outcome of the decay of religious belief. It was an age of cant and shams, so far as the Church and its representatives were concerned. Before bringing in the new age the old one must first be ridiculed. Whenever an institution or a belief can be laughed at, its doom is sealed. Wit and humour, accordingly, as much as religious convictions, play their part in human progress. If they do not build up, they at any rate clear the ground and pave the way for a fresh reconstruction.

The poem which Buchanan wrote, and which to a large extent shaped his future, was the *Somnium*, an elegy which he says he had composed in his leisure hours. What prompted him to write this satire he does not say. The two that succeeded it, we know, were produced at the request of the king.

The opening lines of the poem, and an expression that occurs in *Franciscanus*, would seem to hint that at this time Buchanan was hesitating whether he should enter the Church or not. His future, at best, was very uncertain; his engagement with the Earl of Cassillis was coming to an end. Scotland had very few openings for a man like him. The Church still continued to be the channel for preferment and promotion; it would in any case give him that learned leisure which his soul must have desired. The friars, besides, would naturally wish to capture so promising a recruit; better in any case that he should be on their side than against them. But if Buchanan hesitated, it can only have been for a moment. His worst enemies have never accused him of gross worldliness, and he is the last man that we can conceive sacrificing his deepest convictions for mere earthly gain. The picture of Buchanan as a monk is hard to imagine.

The *Somnium* is a frank imitation, indeed a free translation into Latin, of a poem by Dunbar, entitled " How Dunbar was desyrit to be ane Fryer." The poet describes himself as being visited in a dream by St. Francis, the founder of the Order, who

invites him to become a monk, holding out among
other promises that of heaven. The poet, however,
will have nothing to do with the Saint or his
"hooded crew," whom he describes in no flattering
terms. He has no objections, however, to be a
Bishop; that, he thinks, is an office worth holding.
And so he winds up and dismisses the Saint as
follows:

> "Let others traverse all the country o'er,
>   Proud of this dress and beg from door to door;
>   The trade I like not, nor the monkish frown,
>   Give me a mitre and a purple gown."

This effusion had a twofold result; it drew on
Buchanan the enmity of the Franciscans, and commended him to the attention of the King. The
religious Orders took themselves very seriously;
they must have had the suspicion that their hold
on the people was growing slacker, and they were
constantly on the outlook for any slight that
might affect or endanger their position. They at
once fastened on Buchanan's poem, and as their
manner was when no real charge could be made
against a man, they trumped up one, and the
most common and fatal accusation was to declare

him to be a heretic. It was thus they acted towards Buchanan. In place of terrorising him, however, it but confirmed his opinion of their malice and " licentiousness, and rendered him still more partial to the Lutheran views." The King, too, instead of believing them or being offended by Buchanan's satire, invited the author to become tutor to his natural son, the Lord James Stewart.

James the Fifth was no lover of the Franciscan Order; he believed that at this very time they were involved in a plot which aimed at his own life. He wished also to break the power of the Church, which had grown fat and strong during his long minority. After the battle of Flodden, where his own father and the flower of the nobility had been slain, the government of the country fell into the hands of the Church, with the result that it became a power which it was the aim of wise statesmanship to diminish, if not to crush. For this end he encouraged Sir David Lyndsay to write those satires which ridiculed the clergy, and honoured with his presence and that of his Queen Madeline the representation of one of them, the *Satire of the Three Estates*, in 1539. He accordingly

5

saw in Buchanan a new ally, and advised him to
make a fresh attack on the Franciscans. The poet
felt that in his first effusion he had perhaps gone
far enough, and he determined to write a short poem
susceptible of an "ambiguous interpretation," but
he found that it satisfied neither the King nor the
Franciscans. James demanded something "keen
and biting," which should not only "prick the
skin, but probe the vitals"; and everything
appeared criminal to the Franciscans unless it
were written expressly in their praise. The
"ambiguous" poem is the *Palinodia*, and the
"keen and biting" one, the *Franciscanus*.

Buchanan misjudged the Franciscans if he thought
the two short poems which compose the *Palinodia*
would mitigate their wrath; they increased it ten-
fold. Nor should this surprise us, for if in the
Somnium he chastised them with whips, in the
Palinodia he belaboured them with scorpions. Its
satire is keen and piercing. It describes the poet as
carried to heaven. He suddenly finds himself in a
great hall filled with monks. Their representatives
on earth must have winced at the laughable description which he gives of the appearance of the saintly

friars. The tables, however, are turned, judgment is passed upon the poet, and the divine anger of the holy fraternity is let loose on his devoted head. Stripped of his clothes, they beat him almost to death, and he, to appease their fury, invokes upon their heads all those blessings which their mundane brethren so greatly coveted and enjoyed. " Profane not your holy hands in my blood," he cries. " So may your seraphic Order flourish under ever more glorious auspices. So may the ignorant and the stupid join your tribe in flocks, and may never an old woman be wanting for you to gull. May the mob never discover your lies, nor see through your impostures."

> "Songs, psalms, and concerts, gardens gay with flowers,
>   And gorgeous palaces amuse your hours."

The full fury of Buchanan's invective, however, was reserved for his *Franciscanus*, the longest and most elaborate and finished of all his satires. A draft of it was made, and the only copy was submitted to the King. The poem did not take final shape till after Buchanan's return to Scotland in 1560, when he published it with a dedication to the Earl of Moray. During these long years that it lay beside him, the poet must have repeatedly revised it and given it those touches which place it, so far as style, at least, is concerned, high not only among his own works, but among the satires of the age. A recent critic is of opinion that its "force is weakened by a profusion of details, which never once collects itself in one of the true Juvenalian onslaughts"; while another, accepting it as "a brilliant performance, careful in construction, ingenious in detail, abounding in happy sallies," admits that it is not satire of the type that "rises into poetry by the disinterestedness and the very intensity of its denounciation of evil." "There is nothing," he remarks, "in Buchanan here of the prophet's or reformer's fulness of soul or their burning consciousness of a divine cause." All this may be granted without in any way detracting from the high qualities of the poem. It simply means that the writer was not Juvenal or Knox, but Buchanan, and if the power of his satire is to be judged by its results, the *Franciscanus* does not need to fear comparison. It roused the anger of its victims to such a pitch that the writer ever afterwards was a marked man, and escaped as if by miracle the dire fate they destined for him.

The poem opens with a pleasing description of the Church as the haven of the storm-tossed soul, and a fanciful sketch of the lives of those monks who, by their profession, ought to be the holiest of men. A graphic and telling description is then given of the real Franciscan, startling enough to turn away from the Order any silly youth who believed that within monastic walls he would enjoy a foretaste of the bliss of heaven. It is not pure and devotional natures who join the fraternity, but the lowest types: the sot, the ignorant, the ruined in purse and character, the renegade from justice, the sensualist, the gambler, the glutton. Whence comes the success of such knaves? wherein consists their secret? How do they manage to impose on the world?—Low cunning, the tricks of the profession, and the art of imposition which have been practised for years and brought to the highest pitch of perfection. These the veteran teaches the novice, who is informed that the most powerful weapon at his command will be the Confessional. Worm out the secrets of the penitent, and the

deluded creature will be the friar's victim and
slave ever after. Prospect your ground, choose
your prey—the rich matron, the dull rustic. Do
not be afraid to speak, knowledge is not necessary ;
cultivate effrontery, lard your sermons with a few
Latin phrases, terrify your hearers with the pains
of hell. But a reaction is setting in, the Epistles
of Paul have been rediscovered, truth is beginning
to dawn, and the trade of the Franciscan is
threatened with extinction.

The modern reader who has grown accustomed to
the polite and vacuous literature of the times, may
hold up his hands in horror at what may seem to him
to be the coarseness of much of Buchanan's verse.
But the poet, as we know from the most reliable
authority, simply described what existed. And if
he had written otherwise he would have belied or
suppressed the truth. The Christian world was
rising to a consciousness of its religious and moral
inheritance. The Scriptures were passing from hand
to hand, and the dullest could not fail to observe the
terrible contrast between their teaching and practice
and the doctrines and conduct of the priesthood and
monastic orders. Lyndsay's satires are quite as out-

spoken as Buchanan's, and as he wrote in the
vernacular the sense of the age cannot have been
shocked. Every thinking man knew what was going
on, and all that was needed was a poet like Buchanan,
who would give the thoughts and feelings of the
times literary expression. This he did in his
Franciscanus, which mirrors for succeeding centuries the monastic life of the age.

The Church felt that such men as Buchanan must
be silenced. About the very time when the last
of his series of satires was completed, it took alarm
at the spread of the new opinions, and reached forth
its hand to seize and destroy the disturbers of its
peace. The year 1539 in particular witnessed
vigorous activity on its part against heretics. "In
the beginning of that year," Buchanan tells us,
"many suspected of Lutheranism were seized ;
towards the end of February five were burned, nine
recanted, many were exiled. Among the last was
George Buchanan, who while his guards were asleep
escaped from the window of his sleeping apartment."
This was the work of Cardinal Beaton, and when
Buchanan heard that his arch-enemy had offered
the King a bribe for his capture, he hastened across

the border, and at the hands of Sir John Rainsford
found shelter for a brief time from the thieves, the
plague, and papists, that in his flight threatened to
destroy him.   While in this "famous knight's"
house, which Buchanan says was "an altar of refuge
to the wretched, an ark of safety to the good," he
wrote two short poems, one to Thomas Cromwell,
and another to the King himself.   The tone of
these poems reveals the sore straits in which the
poet now found himself, but despairing of relief from
either quarter, and finding that Henry was "burning
Catholic and Protestant alike on the same day and
in the same fire, and as more intent on safeguarding
his prerogative than advancing pure religion," he
quitted England and sought a home in France,
directing his steps to Paris.

CHAPTER VI

THE DRAMATIST

IT must have been with a shock of surprise that Buchanan learned, on reaching Paris, that Cardinal Beaton was there before him. The eminent Scottish ecclesiastical politician, who was rapidly working his way to the highest position in the public life of his own country, chanced to be in France on an Embassy in the very year of Buchanan's flight from Scotland. Very few countries in Western Europe were at this time safe for such a man as the satirist of the Franciscans. He naturally turned to France, as the home of most of his friends and the scene of his education and early labours. Even its scenery would seem to have inspired him, and to have drawn out his poetic talent more than that of his native country. The love for the grand in nature was of later growth. Two centuries had to pass before full poetic expression would be given to it. The mountains of Scotland sank into insignificance before the plains of France. The Garonne was more to Buchanan than his own Loch Lomond.

France, too, had other attractions for him. Most of the great scholars of the time had passed through the University of Paris and were now acting as teachers in one or other of its Colleges. The literary society, which a man such as he must have found most congenial, could be met with there to a greater extent than elsewhere. It is true that the governing powers in France had begun to set their face in a determined manner against both the new religion and the new learning. Persecutions were taking place up and down the country, but there was a better chance for Buchanan to find some work and to escape the fury of the Franciscans in France than in his native land.

Paris, accordingly, was no safe place for him, and shortly after his arrival he fortunately received an offer which secured him employment and guaranteed his safety. In the year 1533 a great school had been opened in Bordeaux. According to Montaigne, who was one of its earliest pupils, it was "very

flourishing for that time, and the best in France."
It was called the Collége de Guyenne, and had for
its head, André de Gouvéa, who was looked upon as
" the greatest Principal of France." This André
was the nephew of Buchanan's old friend, Jacques de
Gouvéa, under whom he had acted as Regent in
Ste. Barbe. There happened to be two vacancies
at this time in the College. One of them Gouvéa
offered to Buchanan, and the other to his friend Élie
Vinet. Both accepted, and immediately entered upon
their new duties. Here Buchanan remained for
three years, which, from a literary point of view,
were among the most fruitful of his whole life.

This great school of learning was the offspring of
Humanism, and was meant to give embodiment to the
new ideas on education that were then beginning to
prevail. It was a secondary school, and was intended
to take the place, in method at least, of the old
Academy or Grammar School, which was of ancient
foundation in Bordeaux. From the success that
attended, and the interest that was taken in it by
the civic authorities and others, we can note the new
life that was beginning to stir the minds of educationists. Whether the theories which were put into

shape by Gouvéa were right or wrong, he evidently inspired both teachers and scholars with a genuine love of learning.

The Latin language was the chief subject taught. Year after year the pupil was drilled in the study of the great Roman writers, until he could speak with ease in the language of Cicero. Logic, philosophy, Greek, and the Bible had a very secondary place, and scientific and commercial subjects no place at all. The old methods of scholasticism were entirely discarded by Gouvéa and his staff, with some gain no doubt, but not without a considerable loss. The youthful mind cannot live on Latin alone; there are more things in heaven and earth than classical literature. But the spirit which found an outlet in the Collége de Guyenne soon spread over Western Europe, conditioned the course of study in schools and Universities, and still survives. In recent years it has met with strong opposition, and the growth of science, with its practical and utilitarian results, threatens to oust the study of classics from its time-honoured place in our schools of learning. There are extremists on both sides, and it is difficult meanwhile to foresee the issue; but the fact that

Universities ought to aim at producing the highest and widest culture, should never be lost sight of by those who are responsible for education.

The literary activity of Buchanan at this time, to which reference has been made, was no doubt largely due to the congenial surroundings, warm friendships, and social intercourse which he enjoyed. The Principal and Regents would seem to have lived and worked on the best terms with each other; agreeable companions were to be found in the city and neighbourhood, and the bright lads whom the fame of the College drew to it must have made for Buchanan the work of teaching more pleasant than he found it to be when Regent in Ste. Barbe. Among these lads was young Montaigne, who in the course of centuries was to become a European Classic. In one of his most famous essays, that on "the Education of Children," he speaks with the warmest admiration of Buchanan, who was one of his teachers, and whom he characterises as "that great Scotch poet." He remarks that he subsequently met Buchanan, while the latter was acting as tutor to the Count de Brissac, when his distinguished teacher told him that he intended to

write a treatise on education for the benefit of his
pupil, taking Montaigne himself as his example ; but
when Buchanan's work did appear, it failed to satisfy
Montaigne's description of it.

The one man with whom he would seem to have
had the most pleasant intercourse during these years
of schoolmastering at Bordeaux, was the elder
Scaliger. This veritable swashbuckler of letters
had a varied and romantic career. He credited
himself with a royal descent. Born in Italy, he was
driven while still an infant from his native land, and
after a youth of trying experiences he took up the
rôle of a soldier of fortune, and distinguished himself
in various warlike enterprises. He thought, at one
time, of joining the Franciscan Order, and with that
intention studied for two years at the University of
Bologna. His eyes were opened to the folly of the
step he was meditating, and, after further wandering,
he settled at last at Agen, some sixty or seventy
miles from Bordeaux. He had in the interval fallen
in love with a young girl, Andiette de Roques
Loberac, of good family, but her parents objected
to the marriage on the ground of his uncertain
prospects. He studied medicine, prosecuted his

suit, became physician to the Bishop of Agen, and married Andiette. During most of this time he had been working hard at Latin and Greek, and became a remarkable classical scholar.

Finding the society of Agen somewhat limited, Scaliger became friendly with the learned men of Bordeaux, and particularly with the Regents of the Collége de Guyenne, who were in the habit of spending their autumn holidays at his house in Agen. Buchanan and he grew intimate, interchanged poems, and entertained the highest regard for each other to the very end. It is interesting to find two such men maintaining so close a friendship with each other, for Scaliger was of a violent temperament, and Buchanan's wit was severe and sharp. The Scotchman could not fail to admire Scaliger's manly independence, and the Italian had the highest appreciation of Buchanan's ability, scholarship, and poetical gifts. Joseph Scaliger, the younger, was only a boy of ten at this time, but he grew up to be a much more distinguished man than his father, and to entertain even a higher opinion of his father's friend. In after years he paid the highest tribute to Buchanan's poetry in the well-known sentence,

" Buchanan is the one poet in the whole of Europe,
leaving in Latin poetry all others behind." And in
the Elegy which he wrote on Buchanan he is equally
laudatory and happy.

> " Raised to her zenith, poetry no more
>   Beyond thee tries on daring wing to soar,
>   Bounds to her Empire, Rome in Scotland found,
>   And Scotland too her eloquence shall bound."

Bordeaux, while Buchanan was resident there, was
honoured by a visit from Charles the Fifth. The
Collége de Guyenne, determining not to be behind
in welcoming the august visitor, presented him with
a Latin Ode. The man selected to write it was
Buchanan. The choice was a signal tribute to his
gifts, and he acquitted himself to the satisfaction
of everyone. The funds of the College being in a
somewhat uncertain condition, the Chancellor of the
kingdom was approached. He, too, had to be addressed in a Latin Ode. This honour again fell to
Buchanan. Other occasional pieces were composed
by him at this time, some serious, some humorous.
Among the latter was a satire on the brothers of
St. Anthony at Bordeaux, who enjoyed the privilege
of free trade in pigs. The sacred fraternity took

full advantage of their immunity from taxation and filled their monastery with swine, which of course they could dispose of at a high profit. Their traffic, however, becoming a nuisance and a danger to the public health, the magistrates endeavoured to put it down. This gave occasion to Buchanan for the following epigram :

"When living, thou St. Anthony
    As swine-herd kept thy swine,
Now dead, thou keep'st, St. Anthony,
    This herd of monks of thine.

"The monks as stupid are as they,
    As fond of dirt and prog ;
In dumbness, torpor, ugliness,
    Each Monk is like each hog.

"So much agrees 'tween herd and herd,
    One point would make all good ;
If, but thy monks, St. Anthony,
    Had acorns for their food."

More serious subjects, however, engaged Buchanan's leisure hours. He himself tells us that it was with the distinct purpose of elevating the taste of the scholars, as much as in keeping with the practice of the College, that he composed four dramas, which with varying degree of excellence added greatly to

6

his reputation. The French in particular had for many years been addicted to the witnessing of allegories and mystery plays, which, in addition to being written in the vernacular, were repellent to the Humanists from their grossness of ideas and barbarous language. Italian scholars had previous to this time produced a number of Latin dramas, and Erasmus, among others, had translated several Greek plays. The Collége de Guyenne, which was taking the lead in French secondary education, set itself to reform the public taste, and Buchanan, from his already proved poetical gifts and ripe scholarship, was selected to take his turn in producing Latin plays which should be acted by the scholars. Four dramas were accordingly written by him, two of which were translations from Euripides, and two original. These plays have been differently criticised. Competent writers praise them highly; others, while admiring their sonorous verse, affect to disparage them, particularly the original ones, because of their lack of dramatic interest. Buchanan himself did not attach very great importance to them. He admits that the two which he translated, the *Medea* and *Alcestis* of Euripides, were undertaken chiefly as an exercise in turning Greek into Latin. In this way he believed he would acquire a more perfect knowledge of the former language, which he was teaching himself. His success with the *Alcestis* was so great that his contemporaries believed that it was the work of Ennius, who was known to have translated this play. Buchanan they thought had discovered it, and published it in his own name.

It is of course by his two original plays, the *Baptistes* and *Jephthes*, that he must stand or fall as a dramatist. A recent critic finds in them an imitation of Seneca rather than of Euripides, and a general lack of dramatic interest and movement. Others see in them allusions, such as references to Greek characters and names, which are glaring improprieties in works that have a purely Scriptural basis. While this may be true, the credit should not be denied to Buchanan of excelling his contemporaries in such compositions and of writing dramas, which, notwithstanding the limitations under which they were written, can still be read with interest. No one can fail to see the opportunity which the story of Jephthah gives for

dramatic handling. The conflicting emotions in
the breast of the father because of his rash vow,
the agony of the mother and the renunciation of
the daughter, battling with the natural love of life,
are intensely human and realistic. Buchanan, it
must be admitted, rose to the height of his theme,
and his *Jephthes* easily takes its place among productions of its class.

A singular interest attaches to his other original
play, the *Baptistes*. It and the *Medea* were his
first ventures in this species of composition, and it
was their success that encouraged him to write the
other two. The interest of the *Baptistes* lies in
its subject and characters rather than in its dramatic
treatment. It was a parable for the times, and its
readers would not fail to see the significance of
its allusions. In it we have the first sketch of
Buchanan's views of government, which were afterwards fully developed in his " History " and in his
famous tract, *De Jure Regni apud Scotos*. It is
interesting to note that at this early period of
his career he had formed those opinions on a
limited monarchy and the rights of the people
which afterwards distinguished him and made him

a leader in constitutional reform. The selection of
John the Baptist for dramatic treatment lent itself
admirably to the embodiment of the views which
he then and ever afterwards cherished. So pronounced, indeed, are these views, that his chief
biographer thinks that the play could not have been
acted at that time in Bordeaux, for the offence it
would have given. Buchanan himself would seem
to indicate differently, and one would be glad to
believe that Montaigne represented one of its
characters, as he certainly did some others of
Buchanan's, for he tells us that " he played the chief
parts in the Latin tragedies of Buchanan, Guérente,
and Muret, which were represented in the Collége
de Guyenne with dignity."

The theme of the *Baptistes* is the great one of
human liberty, and the poet speaks out with the
utmost boldness against tyranny and priestcraft.
Its leading characters would find their modern
instances : John the Baptist, say, in Luther ; Malchus
the high priest, in Cardinal Beaton ; Herod, in Francis
the First or James the Fifth of Scotland ; and
Herodias in Louise of Savoy, the Queen-Mother. In
1642 it was translated into English, and at that time,

when rebellion was in the air, its readers would discover Charles the First in Herod; Laud, in Malchus; and Henrietta Maria, in Herodias. In the Dedication to James the Sixth, with which Buchanan prefaced the edition of 1576, he remarks: " It is my desire that this little book may be for a testimony to posterity, that if at any time, whether at the instigation of evil counsellors or from the licence of sovereignty overbearing a good education, you should in any way misconduct yourself, the blame is to be imputed not to your teachers but to yourself, as having not obeyed their salutary admonitions." James was at this time his pupil, and to make clear what these admonitions, as illustrated by the *Baptistes*, were, he in the same letter of dedication observes: " But that in this little work, which more particularly concerns you, is its clear exhibition of the torments of tyrants and the miseries which they endure, even when they seem to be most prosperous."

We have no record of the reason which induced Buchanan to leave Bordeaux. There is no evidence that it was the fear of persecution. Cardinal Beaton, it is true, had not forgotten him, for he sent a letter to the Archbishop of Bordeaux desiring the poet's

apprehension. The communication fortunately fell
into the hands of Buchanan's greatest friends, and
consequently failed in its object. Beaton now had
his hands full, for James the Fifth was dead, and
he was aiming at the chief power in the State. It
may have been the love of change that possessed
Buchanan, like the other wandering scholars of the
time, that induced him to leave Bordeaux. We
cannot tell, but either at the close of 1542 or early
in 1543 he departed from the city.

CHAPTER VII

BIOGRAPHERS of Buchanan have experienced considerable difficulty in tracing his steps for the next five years. Certain of them, misapprehending the phrase *precepteurs domestiques* which Montaigne employs in referring to Buchanan, imagine that, after leaving Bordeaux, he became private tutor to that young scholar and resided with him at his father's house. This was not the case, for the phrase only implies that he was one of Montaigne's masters while teaching in the Collége de Guyenne. In 1544, however, we learn that he was acting as Regent in the Collége du Cardinal Lemoine in Paris. This College was one of the most progressive in the University, and would naturally welcome a liberal-minded man like Buchanan. He had as colleagues some of the most distinguished

scholars in Europe, notably Turnébe and Muret.
They, along with Buchanan, held at this time the
first place in the scholastic world, and about them,
as a contemporary observed, there was "nothing of
the pedagogue except the gown and cap." He
had also other associates of outstanding distinction,
and to two who were his fellow-workers at Bordeaux
he wrote an elegy which is full of biographical
interest. It not only informs us of the writer's
habitation at this time, and the condition of his
fortunes, but also throws light on a side of his
character, which is all the more attractive because
it is not the one that is usually regarded as typical
of Buchanan's life as a whole. When he wrote
this elegy he was clearly suffering from a painful
and dangerous malady, or rather a complication of
maladies, which threatened to have a fatal ending.

We can picture the lonely scholar, far from his
native land, with prospects uncertain, lying on a
sick-bed and looking forward to a speedy dissolution.
He had now turned forty, and was still without a
permanent appointment; he was also unmarried,
and without those ministrations from wife and
children which alleviate suffering, and comfort the

troubled heart. But this poem comes upon us
with a welcome surprise, and shows us that he was
far from friendless. Indeed, he would seem to have
been visited daily by colleagues and companions
whose affection he had won, and who cheered him
by their friendly intercourse. There must have
been something in Buchanan more than the grim
humorist and biting satirist to have drawn to him,
in the closest bonds of friendship, so many men
whose esteem was an honour. These and others,
whose regard he afterwards gained, ever spoke and
wrote of him in the highest terms as a man, a
scholar, and a poet.

After describing the nature of the malady from
which he was suffering, he continues: "Such are
the dire images of death and death-bringing want
that visit me. Nor by my side have I my Tastæus
and Tevius, whose pleasant converse would make
the long day short. Neither is my sick heart
refreshed by the learning and eloquence of my other
friends of the Gascon school. Yet amid all my ills,
tried friends have not wholly deserted me. Often
Groscollius expounds to me the virtues of his herbs
and helps to cheer me by his kind counsel. Often

the skill and experience of Carolus Stephanus brings
relief to my suffering. Turnebus, that pride of the
Muses, suffers not a day to pass without the offices
of friendship. And though other blessings fail me,
the pious care of my comrade Gelida supplies the
place of father and fatherland alike. While it is
day my lot is thus made light. With the coming
of night an army of cares raise their sighs around
me, and a thousand shapes haunt my dreams. In
the silence of the darkness your forms come before
me and make the night watches short with beguiling
words. Yet though vain and all too brief is this
delight, 'tis sweet, even thus, to know the presence
of those we love. Perchance also in the dreams of
the night I may ghostlike stand by your couch, and
in words mingled with sighs bewail the hardness of
my untoward lot. And ye dreams, sweetest pledges
of the night, let not grief for me touch my absent
friends; alone let me bear the burden of my fate.
But if inexorable doom shall move me hence before
my day, late may the tale reach the ears of my
Tastæus and Tevius. And ye of one mind and one
soul cease from tears, and grieve me not with your
lament when I am gone."

Buchanan recovered, and in the following year, 1545, he left Paris. We then lose sight of him till two years afterwards, when he set out for Portugal, whither he had been invited by his former chief, André de Gouvéa, to assist at the establishing of a great school of learning in Coimbra, whose University had recently been founded by King John the Third. This monarch, who in the earliest part of his reign was an enlightened patron of letters, was most eager to see in his own country a University that would rank with the very best in Europe. He accordingly invited Gouvéa to return to his native land to take charge of the Institution. The great Principal responded, and set out for Portugal accompanied by Buchanan and a number of other distinguished scholars, most of whom had been associated with him at the Collége de Guyenne. It was in March 1547 that this notable band of Humanists sailed for Coimbra, and so hopeful was Buchanan of the prospects thus opened out to him, that he persuaded his brother Patrick to accompany him as a member of the teaching staff. Everything went well at first, and the new University gave every promise of success and of drawing to it the young Portuguese students who had formerly been accustomed to repair to Paris for the education which their own country could not provide. This, indeed, was one of the chief objects of the King. An event, however, took place which shattered all these hopes, and entailed much persecution and suffering on Buchanan. In 1548, a year after he had gone to Portugal, the great Principal died, and after his death the Jesuits, who at this early date had found their way into the country and acquired great influence over the King, used every means to dispossess Gouvéa's Regents and to gain the control of the University themselves. The dogs of persecution were let loose on Buchanan and his friends. They were charged with crimes invented by their accusers for the occasion. Three of them were thrown into dungeons; after a lengthened imprisonment they underwent a mock trial, and were again committed to prison.

The relentless bigotry of these inquisitors found its chief victim in Buchanan. From the way in which he refers to this part of his career it can be seen that the iron had entered his soul, and that this persecution made a more lasting impression upon him than any other to which he was subjected

during his whole life. His chief ground of offence
would seem to have been the poem which he wrote
against the Franciscans. His accusers could have
known of that poem only by hearsay, and he had
stipulated with the King, before he agreed to come
to Portugal, that it would not be brought up against
him. He was also accused of eating flesh in Lent,
of having spoken disparagingly of monks, of having
quoted St. Augustine as being in favour of the
Reformed doctrine of the Eucharist, and two
witnesses deponed that they had ground for believing that he was no good Catholic. " But to be
brief," as he himself remarks, " when the inquisition
had fatigued both themselves and him nearly a year
and a half, at last, that they might not seem wantonly
to have harassed to no purpose one not altogether
unknown to fame, they shut him up for some months
in a monastery to be more strictly instructed by the
monks, some of whom were neither altogether
deficient in humanity, learning, or morals, but all
were destitute of religion. During this confinement
he chiefly employed himself in versifying the Psalms
of David in a variety of measures."

This incident instinctively calls up to one's mind

the editing by John Knox, while he was a slave in
the French galleys, of Balnave's treatise on Justification. The two greatest Scotsmen of their time were
almost in the very same year incarcerated, the one
in a Portuguese dungeon, and the other in a French
man-of-war. And yet neither of them lost one jot
of hope or heart. In place of being crushed by
their hard fate, they wrested from it the means of
religious and mental liberty. " Surely it would be
difficult to find a more dramatic position even in that,
the heroic period, as it may truly be called of modern
literary history ! Here was a Scot from the Lennox
—born hard by the river Blane, amidst the lochs and
mountains of the North—imprisoned among lemon-
complexioned monks under the sun of Lusitania,
and while nominally undergoing their illiterate
teaching, beguiling the hours by founding a great
classical religious work. But there is something
more than dramatic in the picture of Buchanan
translating the Psalms in a Portuguese cell. His
great nature had known sorrow and was feeling it
now, like the Royal Psalmist himself ; and if he cried
to his Lord in a language which was not that he
had learned from his mother, the intellectual labour

did not, we may feel sure, altogether deaden the spiritual pain. The translation, thus viewed, had a special moral interest, and the fact that such were Buchanan's occupations prepares us for finding him by and by one of the founders of modern Protestant Scotland, along with the Regent Moray and Knox."

Buchanan at length was set at liberty, and he asked permission to return to France. "The King, however, wished him to remain, and supplied him with means sufficient for his daily wants. But sick of delays and uncertain hopes, he embarked at Lisbon in a Cretan ship and sailed for England." He arrived at an unfortunate time ; the country was in a most disturbed condition ; the war of religion which still raged was being complicated and intensified by a war of succession. Northumberland, who divided the power with Somerset, was advocating the claims of his son's wife, the Lady Jane Grey, to the throne. Times had changed since the days when Erasmus found a welcome asylum in England during the reign of Henry the Eighth. A country distracted by internal feuds was no home for a quiet scholar, so, after a sojourn of a few months, Buchanan, early in 1553, crossed the channel for his beloved France and Paris.

Nor did France at first sight offer a safer home for him than England. Under Henry the Second it was plunged into foreign wars, and its domestic affairs were disturbed by a bitter religious persecution. The Protestants were burned and banished; and it might seem a bold step for so well known a man as Buchanan to put himself into such imminent peril. It ought, however, to be remembered that up till this time he had not declared for the Reformed religion. He was outwardly still a Romanist, and to the world he was known as a Humanist, who enjoyed the privilege of satirising the clergy and exposing the abuses of the Roman Church without being subjected to the persecution which dogged the steps of the heretic. It is only on such grounds that Buchanan's immunity from the fate that befell the followers of Luther at this time in France can be explained, but it is not at all unlikely that even though he had been conscious of danger he would have risked much in order to find himself in France once more. It was the home of his adoption, of his friends, of his early labours and first literary achieve-

7

ments.   He loved, too, its fertile plains, its vine-shaded
hills, its richly watered valleys and far-sweeping
rivers.   " Happy France," he exclaims in one of the
best and brightest of his poems, " with thy sweet
country homes, thy ramparted walls, thy stately
castles, and thy sons adorned with all the graces of
life, modest, courteous, and pleasant of speech. . . .
France ! if while I live I love and cherish thee not,
as one loves and cherishes the land of his birth,
then may I return to the barren wastes and niggard
soil of Portugal."

The poet's love for France, deep though it was,
found its full satisfaction in his passion for Paris.
Johnson's love for London has its parallel in
Buchanan's intense admiration of the city on the
Seine. The emotion which the thought of Paris
created in his breast found fit expression in one of
the very finest of his poems, *Desiderium Lutetiæ*.   In
this ode, written in Portugal, he pours forth his
regrets at his prolonged absence from the city of
his heart, which he invokes as " Fair Amaryllis."
Seven summers with their furnace heat, and seven
winters with their storms and clouds, have parted
him from her gaze.

"Thou art my theme when in the dewy morn
The cattle crop the herbage; and again
'Neath noontide sweltering glare thou'rt still my theme;
And when the nightfall lengthens out the shades,
E'en night which wraps creation all in gloom,
May by no spell thy sweet face hide from me."

His sleep is disturbed by fleeting dreams and vain
visions of the city that he loves, and with the
breaking of the day his sorrow drives him to the
Fields and Woods, to whom he tells his plaints.

"Full often hang I on a mountain crag
That looks upon the sea—the billowy sea:
And, wild with frenzy, call the dark blue waves
And gales that will not hear me—woe is me!
O ocean, and ye nymphs that cleave the waves—
Ye Nereid nymphs that cleave the glassy waves—
Be kind, and waft me to the port I love."

He invokes the gales that blow to the south-west
to bring him tidings of his Love, and calls upon
the east wind to be the messenger of his hopes and
fears.

"How oft when Eurus, light, came skimming by
I've called to him, 'Say hast thou seen my Love.
O happy Gale! say does she think of me?
Say is her passion deep as mine for her?
Say can'st thou mark in her the ancient flame?'
He blusters past, and soughing, passes by
Like to an angry man, and leaves me dumb."

Spain and Portugal under the forms of Lycisca and
Melænis, two maidens, try to woo him from his
ancient Love, but in vain.

> "Oft pale Melænis in the mirror lake
> 　Hath taught her beauteous form to look its best:
> 　Painted her eyes and trick'd her raven locks,
> 　And yearn'd in vain to merit beauty's meed.
> 　Oft she has cried, ' Poor Daphnis, silly boy,
> 　Why pine for love of one who's far away?
> 　My land can give thee all thy soul can wish.
> 　The grapes are purple: cull them ere they fall!'
> 　Oft, too, Lycisca when some festal train
> 　Swept by her windows (I among the rest),
> 　Would turn her head and would not see me pass;
> 　She then would stamp and clash the cymbals loud,
> 　And sing of Nemesis who bides her time—
> 　Sing of revenge for unrequited love."

They warn the poet that in despising them, he may
lose both them and his fair Amaryllis as well, but
ever to their strains he closed his ears, and thus
concludes:

> "But dogs with wolves shall mate and bulls with bears,
> 　The hare shall court the fox, the lion the roe,
> 　Before Lycisca with her cymbals clang,
> 　Or yet Melænis with her winning ways
> 　May steal my passion from my ancient love.
> 　She who with. love has known to fire my heart,
> 　Shall know my heart's on fire until I die."

Buchanan arrived in France in the beginning of 1553, about the time the siege of Metz was raised, and was constrained by his friends to write a poem on the occasion, which he did with reluctance, being unwilling to enter into competition with a number of his acquaintances, particularly Melin de St. Gelais, whose learned and elegant eulogy was at that time in circulation. For the next two years he resided in Paris, and acted for a time as Regent in the Collége Boncourt. At the end of this period he entered upon what would seem to have been the happiest and most fruitful engagement in his life. He had many friends in the highest ranks of society who admired his talents and afforded him protection, but with none had he more pleasant relations than with the eminent soldier, Charles du Cossé, Comte de Brissac, one of the marshals of France, in whose family he was to be an honoured inmate for the next five years. Buchanan seems to have known de Brissac prior to this period, and to have received some recognition at his hands ; at all events he addressed to the Marshal a very fine ode on his capture of Vercelli. This was in 1553, and on the 27th of July of the following year, he dedicated to the Count his *Jephthes*.

In his preface to that work, Buchanan has some very handsome things to say of his distinguished patron, and from all that we know of the Marshal's character, he thoroughly deserved them. De Brissac was one of the great men of his time; there was something noble and generous in his nature, and his humanising influence on the methods of warfare then in vogue stamp him as a man far in advance of his age. His noble nature appealed to the poet, and drew out of him all that was best. There must have been something equally remarkable in the character of Buchanan to have induced de Brissac to select him from all the scholars of France to be tutor to his son. This was the post to which the poet was now appointed, and he discharged its duties not only with his usual distinction, but with a whole - heartedness which showed that he was amid congenial surroundings, and in love with his task.

We have already had occasion to refer to Buchanan's love of the soldier's calling, and quoted this same preface to his *Jephthes* in illustration of it.

He looked upon the great military hero as the performer of those noble deeds which fired the poet's muse and supplied the material for his art. The great man, according to Buchanan, is a specialist only by accident, his sympathies go out to greatness wherever it is to be found. He has a natural kinship to scholarship as to everything else that is worthy, and, calling to mind the most famous soldiers of ancient times, he remarks: "All the Generals of every age who have done famous deeds, have been either themselves most learned men or have bestowed the deepest affection upon such as were distinguished for their learning." Such a hero he would seem to have found in de Brissac, especially in his relations to himself. "For," continues the poet, "before you had even seen me, and when I was altogether unknown to you, save by repute, as a scholar, you have so cherished me with all the offices of kindness and generosity, that should my genius yield any fruit, should there be vouchsafed any offspring, as it were, to my vigils, then with justice it should redound to you."

There is a story told of Buchanan's connection with de Brissac which illustrates the other side of the poet's thesis, that war and poetry are kin. "The Marshal," so runs the tale, "was in the habit of admitting George Buchanan, the tutor of his son, to his councils of war. He was led to do this from the following incident. On a certain occasion Buchanan had come down from his bedroom to the dining-room to give some order to a domestic. As it happened, de Brissac, with his staff, was deliberating in an adjoining hall on matters of the gravest importance. Buchanan, overhearing what was said, muttered some words of disapproval. De Brissac noticing a smile on the face of one of his officers, and the reason being given, Buchanan was called in and asked for his opinion. This he did with such sagacity that all present agreed that his suggestions should be adopted. As it happened, the result confirmed the wisdom of Buchanan's counsel."

The tutor had much credit with his young pupil, Timoleon du Cossé. He was only twelve years of age when he came under Buchanan's charge, and he grew up to be a distinguished member of the French nobility, and gave every promise of a successful career. He was unfortunately slain in early manhood. When only twenty-six years of age, he was killed by a musket ball at the siege of Mucidan. It was as a memorial to him that Buchanan undertook the most ambitious of all his poems, *De Sphæra*, upon which he believed his fame would rest, but which was never completed. This was his chief literary venture during his engagement with de Brissac. The soldier was continually on the move between France and Italy. Buchanan accompanied him, and the unsettled life may not have been conducive to literary activity. But it is clear that his mind was beginning to run in another channel.

Up till now his interests were chiefly Humanistic. While perfectly conscious of the defects and abuses of the Roman Church, he had not separated himself from its communion. He now, however, began to give himself to a serious consideration of the grounds on which the Reformed religion was based, and to satisfy himself as to their truth. He had reached the turning-point in his life, and his future career was to be conditioned by the result of his reflection. " A great part of this time," he himself says, " he devoted to the study of the Holy Scriptures, that he might be able to judge correctly respecting those controversies which occupied the greater part of the world, and then began to be set at rest in his own country, now liberated from the tyranny of the Guises. Having returned thither he joined the Scottish Church."

CHAPTER VIII

THE POET

I T may not be inopportune at this stage to consider the poetry of Buchanan. It is quite true that he had not up till now published much verse in a formal manner. What he had written had found its way to the public in detached fragments. These, as they appeared, had passed from hand to hand, and were certainly well enough known to his learned contemporaries, but with one or two exceptions he had not gathered his pieces together and appealed to the world. After his return to Scotland, however, with a more assured position and greater leisure, he set himself, in response chiefly to the entreaties of friends, to collect his poetical effusions. His work as a poet was by this time practically over. The latter part of his life was devoted to public affairs and to his prose writings. He occasionally threw off short pieces, and he may have worked intermittently at *De Sphœra*, the longest and most ambitious of all his poems, but apart from that no verse of much importance or significance came from his pen.

It was undoubtedly as a poet that Buchanan was chiefly known to his contemporaries, and on his supreme distinction in this sphere his great fame rested. It may not be easy, at this time of day, to fully appreciate his unique position among the Humanists of the sixteenth century, indeed it is difficult for many to appraise Humanism itself at its true value. The modern poets who wrote in Latin have suffered a twofold fate : they are neglected by those who love the ancient Classics, and also by those who admire the literature of the vernacular. They rode on the wave of a movement which gave hopes of being permanent and universal; its spirit has survived, but the form in which it was clothed has all but vanished. The intellectual freedom which it so nobly vindicated has gone on increasing, but the Latin tongue in which it was so eloquently sung is, for all literary purposes, as silent as the grave.

Buchanan's friends and contemporaries spoke and wrote of his poetry in the highest and warmest manner. The greatest scholars and critics placed him first in the first rank. Thus Henri Estienne, the most learned printer of his own and perhaps of any age, and a critic of no mean power, said that he was easily the first poet of his time— "poetarum nostri sæculi facile princeps." The two Scaligers, father and son, were equally enthusiastic. They were both severe critics, especially the father, who saw little to his taste even in Erasmus, but they were sincere in their admiration of Buchanan. Joseph the son, who held the first place as a critic among all the scholars of his time, declared "that in Latin poetry Buchanan stood alone in Europe, and left everybody else behind." His epitaph on Buchanan is equally emphatic, and in its concluding lines—

> " Imperii fuerat Romani Scotia limes ;
> Romani eloquii Scotia finis erit ? "

he indicates that in his opinion Buchanan "had brought Latin poetry to a pitch of perfection beyond which it could not go ; and that as Scotland had in the past been the last line of expansion

for the Roman Empire, so in the future it would
in the person of Buchanan be found to have given
the highest note of Roman eloquence." Down
even to the time of Dr. Johnson this view was
the one generally entertained by European scholars.
Indeed, the great dictator himself was almost as
enthusiastic in his admiration of Buchanan as
Estienne and Scaliger. He declares that our
poet was "the only man of genius his country
ever produced," and that he was "not only a very
fine poet, but a great poetical genius." We need
not be surprised that praise of this kind should
have created a certain opposition, and set critics
to discover flaws in the poetry of Buchanan.
Shortly after his death his pre-eminence began to
be disputed, and, strange to say, his rival was a
fellow-countryman, Arthur Johnson. It was inevitable that a reaction should set in ; this is the
fate of even the very greatest.

Hallam, who voiced this reaction, in a moderate
and hesitating way, while he admits Buchanan's
distinction, refuses to accept the unqualified terms
in which Joseph Scaliger and other critics have
spoken of him. Even his translation of the Psalms

he thinks is overpraised. This note has been struck in a higher key by the latest of Buchanan's critics, Professor Saintsbury, who evidently belongs to the school of Mariolaters, that sees the poetry of Buchanan in the distorted light of their false worship. Because Buchanan formed his own opinion of Queen Mary's conduct, and was decided in his action against her, his poetry, forsooth, is poisoned at its very source! Hence Mr. Saintsbury's judgment. "Taking Buchanan's prose and verse together, it may even be doubted whether he had very much literary faculty beyond vigour and the knack of copying the ancients. In other words, both the heaviest curses of the rhetorician are on him; for if he had some skill in making the worse appear the better reason, he was still more often occupied in giving an appearance of existence and even of beauty to what had no reason to exist and no right to be beautiful." Against this may be set the opinion of James Hannay, who in this particular field must be held to be quite as trustworthy a guide as Professor Saintsbury. " As a scholar merely," remarks Mr. Hannay, " Buchanan was a match for any man; but the greatness of

many scholars ended where his had still a new
world before him. He was not only a critic,
philologer, or Latin stylist, but a man of genius,
using the accomplishments which these titles imply
as the tools of a fine intellect. The orations of
Muretus, for instance, are still worth reading by
anybody who cares to see with what easy grace
a dead language may be used by a man of parts
and scholarship. But that exhausts their praise,
for there is no mind at bottom worth the skill
employed in the superficial expression. The
classicism of Muretus is a Roman mask, but a
mask only. The classicism of Buchanan is a Roman
face with a strong living brain behind it."

These two opinions may, according to the views
of different readers, appear somewhat extreme. The
candid mind is apt to revolt against too high praise
or too great depreciation. There can be no question, however, of Buchanan's strong mental force,
rising to genius even, of his exact and wide scholarship, of his poetic gifts and apt literary expression.
There can be no doubt that had he found his native
tongue a fit vehicle for his thoughts and emotions,
he would still be largely read by his fellow-country-

men, and very probably have attained to the position of a modern English classic. It was his fate to have to make use of the Latin tongue, and even his most hostile critics have to admit that he did so with a power and mastery which place him above all his contemporaries, and give him a rank almost equal to some of the Romans themselves.

One is equally surprised at the wide range of Buchanan's interest, and the excellence which he attained in every form of poetic effort attempted by him. We have already seen the signal success which he achieved by his satires and dramas. An ordinary writer might have rested content with the laurels which he thus gained. But these only form a fraction of his writings in verse. From his student days in Paris until his old age he was in the habit of throwing off epigrams and epitaphs, most of them pointed and stinging, and others breathing the spirit of friendship and charity. He thus in a couplet characterised Pope Pius:

"Heaven he sold for money; earth he leaves in death as well:
What remains to Pontiff Pius?—nothing that I see but hell."

Our next quotation, the well-known distich on

8

Zoilus, while equally characteristic, is not quite so grim in its humour.

> "I praise thee Zoilus in vain,
>   In vain you rail at me always;
>   Because the world don't care a grain,
>   What either of the couple says."

The poems, however, which have given rise to most discussion and have provoked the severest criticism, not because of their manner but their subject, are his erotic verses. There could be no harm in the poet pouring forth his soul in amatory stanzas, but those he addressed to Leonora are in the eyes of some so objectionable as to condemn him absolutely. It must frankly be admitted that the character of Leonora as depicted by the poet is sufficiently revolting, and his abuse of her is certainly wholehearted. The friends of Buchanan have not been slow in defending him, and justifying these productions. One broad historical fact should, in handling this question, be kept clearly in view. The poet in writing such verses was only following the custom of the times. Every writer who was ambitious of success strove, during the period of the Renaissance, to imitate the great writers of antiquity at every point, and as their further aim was to attain perfection as Latin stylists, the turning of love ditties, after the most approved manner of the ancients, was a task which they were eager to face and in which they were anxious to excel. Their great masters in this art were Horace, in certain moods, Catullus, and Tibullus. Readers of the Classics need not be told of the objectionable features, from the moral point of view, which appear in the amatory verses of these great poets. And the Humanists, while in all likelihood as fully conscious of their defects as we can be, felt themselves under the literary necessity of imitating and copying them.

It is now generally believed that Phyllis, Amaryllis, Leonora, Neæra, Candida, and the other fair *amorosas* on whom Buchanan, like the other poets of the Renaissance, wrote erotic verses, were purely imaginary characters. They were the creation of the poet's brain, and supplied him with themes on which he might pour forth his scorn or love, as the case might be; at any rate, they gave him the chance of showing his powers as a master of wit and phrases. Most of these poems were simply exercises in Latin verse, and were intended to show off the special gifts of the poet. While this on the whole may be true, these amatory poems reveal the wide gulf that now yawned between the old world and the new. We cannot conceive the great poets of the Middle Ages—Dante, Petrarch, or even the Troubadours—writing in the style of Buchanan and his contemporaries, of those fair beings, real or imaginary, who might provoke their muse. That idealisation of woman fostered by the Church and glorified by the romantic spirit and poetry of Mediævalism, had given place to a realism which, frank and even brutal, faced the world as it is, and was not ashamed to look at and depict its depravity and grossness. It is needless to debate whether human culture has gained or lost by this movement. The literature of modern Europe is a sufficient answer.

Many of Buchanan's friends are at great pains to prove that the licence which he allowed himself in these poems is no evidence of a laxity in his life. Apart altogether from the fact that no charge, or whisper even, of easy morals was ever made against him, the point of view from which, as we have just indicated, the Humanists regarded such verses should be a sufficient reply. Beza, who in his early youth wrote and published a volume of amatory poems, which he dedicated to Melchior Wolmar, a grave and learned man, deliberately declares that though his Muse was loose, his life was chaste. The same can surely be said of Buchanan. But a recent writer goes farther, and justifies the poet in publishing these erotic verses, and tries to show that they are in spirit quite of a piece with his other writings and character. "As far as honesty and consistency go," says Mr. Robert Wallace, "there is no reason why an honest and consistent man should not have written every word of these 'Lena' sketches. Even from an artistic point of view they will stand inspection. The subject, of course, is a revolting one, and so is Dame Quickly,—but would any man of average robustness of mind wish Dame Quickly unwritten? Many people seem to forget that while the real itself may be unpleasant, the artistic image of the real may be a delight. We should shrink from Caliban in the flesh, but Shakespeare throws a charm over him; Pandemonium, I believe, is not a sweet scene, but Milton's account of it is sublime; Falstaff was disreputable, but he makes an admirable stage figure; a corpse is an unlovely object, but

Rembrandt's ' Dissectors ' has a fascination." This is
well said, and not a few will agree with the same
writer when he remarks: " I demur to any sugges-
tion that these or any of Buchanan's so-called
' amorous ' poetry are corrupting, or intended to be,
or that they exhibit any gloating over the degrading
or the degraded on the part of the writer. From
references in them I believe they were satires, written
for the warning of college youth, and resembled
certain passages in the Book of Proverbs and elsewhere in the Bible, where certain counsels highly
necessary and practical are conveyed in language
not deficient either in directness or detail."

Buchanan's verses of this class are not all of the
same savage texture. Some of them, especially
those addressed to Neæra, are light and bright and
playful. The best known are the famous lines of
which Ménage used to say, that " he would have
given his best benefice to have written them," and
Ménage, it is added, held some fat ones.

> " Neæra is harsh at our every greeting,
>   Whene'er I am absent, she wants me again ;
>   'Tis not that she loves me or cares for our meeting,
>   She misses the pleasure of seeing my pain."

One of Buchanan's finest poems is the Ode which he wrote on the marriage of the Dauphin with Queen Mary in 1558. He approved of this marriage, because it bound closer the union between his native country and his beloved France. Great as his admiration was for the land of his adoption, he was a true patriot, and declared that the Dauphin through this marriage was even a greater gainer than the Queen of Scots. There are many passages in the poem worth quoting. We shall give the encomium on his native country, which has become classical:

> " The glory of the quivered Scots
> Is the bold breast and hardy frame
> That fear nor want nor toil can tame;
> Whose joy is in their native woods
> To chase and strike the various game,
> And fearless breast their mountain floods;
> Whose good right hands their soil can keep,
> Nor need high walls nor fosses deep;
> Who count all gone if honour's gone;
> Whose faith can ne'er be bought nor sold;
> Who deem a friend heaven's dearest boon;
> Who barter not their soul for gold.
> So was it when of old, each land
> A prey to every spoiler's hand,
> Its ancient laws and rulers lost,
> The Scot alone could freedom boast!

The Goth, the Saxon, and the Dane,
Poured on the Scot their powers in vain;
And the proud Norman met a foe
Who gave him equal blow for blow.
And I might tell, were not twice-told
The tale, how Rome, whose might controlled
The world beside, was taught to know
That bounds there were she might not pass,
Though never yet had been the foe,
Or man, or nature's direst force,
That e'er had stayed her onward course."

Another of his poems which received the warm approval of no less a master of verse than Wordsworth, is his charming *Calendæ Maiæ*—the First of May. Referring to this poem, James Hannay thinks it was written at Bordeaux, for the poet speaks of the grape which grows on the sandy soil of Gascony. "The poem," he continues, "is full of the images of love and joy and southern merry-making; and like many a quaint passage in Knox's ' History,' and many a brilliant hit in Beza's epigrams, is instructive, as giving us the genial side of those great sixteenth-century Reformers whom wretched modern sentimentalists scarcely ever name without a shudder. Buchanan had heard the chimes at midnight, and the laugh of Neæra in the corner;

and knew well the flavour of Gascon wine, and
talked well over it.   He was earnest and laborious
and proud; but also hilarious and humane."
Wordsworth, writing to his nephew, says: "I think
Buchanan's *Calendæ Maiæ* equal in sentiment, if
not in elegance, to anything in Horace," and Dr.
Hume Brown, whose very fine translation we give,
thinks that "Wordsworth's praise might well have
been more emphatic, and that Buchanan's Ode, by
its true poetic quality, is worthy of Horace when
he transcends himself."

> " Hail ! sweetest day,
>   Day of all pure delight ;
>   Whose gracious hours invite
>   To mirth and song and dance,
>   And wine, and love's soft glance.
>   Welcome ! with all thy bright hours bring
>   Of quickened life and beauty's dower—
>   The certain heritage of Spring.
>   In thee each year doth hoary Time
>   Renew the glories of his prime !
>   When, still rejoicing in her birth,
>   Spring brightened all the new-made earth,
>   And in that happy golden age
>   Men knew no lawless passion's rage,
>   Thy train of joys embraced the year ;
>   Soft breezes wooed the untilled field,
>   Its blessings all unforced to yield.

Even in such mildest atmosphere
Forever bask those happy Isles,
Those blessed plains that never know
Life's slow decay or poisoned flow.
Thus 'mid the still abodes of death
Should steal the soft air's softest breath,
And gently stir the solemn wood
That glooms o'er Lethe's dreamless flood.
And, haply when made pure of stain
By cleansing fire, the earth renewed
Shall know her ancient joys again,
Even such mild air shall o'er her brood!

Thou crown of the world's failing age,
Of life's sad book one happy page.
Hail! sweetest day—memorial bright
Of early innocent delight,
And sure pledge of the coming day
When it shall be eternal May."

The two chief poetical efforts of Buchanan were undoubtedly his *De Sphæra* and his version of the Psalms. Indeed it is upon the latter that his fame as a poet mainly rests. It would seem, however, that he himself believed that it would be by his *De Sphæra* he would attain immortality. Like many others who are the mistaken judges of their own work, he was in this to be disappointed. He began the poem when he was acting as tutor to the young de Brissac, and had evidently written the most of it before his arrival in Scotland. It consists of five books, but the last two were never completed. Buchanan believed that he would secure permanence for his work, both by its subject and the language in which it was written. The system of the heavens, or the mediæval cosmogony of which it treats, provided a theme which to his mind seemed unchangeable, and the Latin language in which he sang its praises, he believed would be the language of literary expression for all time coming. He was disappointed in both hopes; indeed, several years before he began his poem, Copernicus had exploded the Ptolemaic theory of the heavens on which the *De Sphæra* was based, and the rise of the vernacular as the organ of literature in the different countries of Europe had already sounded the death-knell of the Latin tongue.

Buchanan's poem was elaborated with great care, and there are in it passages equal to anything he ever wrote; but the subject lacks interest, and of all his productions it was the one which laid the least hold even on the cultured mind. All the same, Hallam holds it to be the best of his poems, but in this opinion he stands almost alone. The

work which undoubtedly secured for Buchanan his
chief distinction during his own lifetime, and
which since then has maintained his fame, was his
Paraphrase of the Psalms. This, as we have seen,
was undertaken during his confinement in the
monastery in Portugal, although it was not
published till a much later date. Specimens of
his translation into Latin verse of the Sacred
Anthology had found their way into the hands of
Henri Estienne and others, who were so much
struck by them that they called for the speedy
publication of the whole work. Buchanan, in
putting his hand to this undertaking, was simply
acting in the spirit of the times. Versions of the
Psalms into Latin verse had been done by Italian
Humanists, and German and French scholars had
also tried their hand at the same task. Several
of these translations were held to be excellent, but
Buchanan's outstripped them all, and by it he
earned the title of the greatest poet of his age.

Hallam quotes the tributes which were paid to
Buchanan's version by his contemporaries and by
the scholars of subsequent centuries, and he himself is not prepared to question Le Clerc when he

calls his translation of the Psalms incomparable, and prefers it much to that by Beza. Even Mr. Saintsbury admits that Buchanan's Paraphrase is sufficiently elegant Latin, but carps at the poet's inability to make a Roman of King David, or, what most will regard as equally impossible, to divest classical words and phrases of their time-honoured associations and make them the unpolluted channels of Hebrew thought and expression. In two instances, at least, Buchanan's work is universally admitted to rise above all criticism; these are his rendering of the hundred and fourth, and the hundred and thirty-seventh Psalms. It may be quite true that his version is free, that he employs a variety of metre altogether unknown to Hebrew Hymnists, and that he makes a completed whole of what in many cases are but broken lyrical breathings, but he displays a keen appreciation of the spirit of his subject and an easy mastery of expression, which produce a pleasing and finished whole. His work formed during the seventeenth and eighteenth centuries a text-book in many of the best schools in Scotland. In summing up his discussion of this portion of Buchanan's literary labours, James Hannay says: " The result is

a work unequal in parts, too closely recalling sometimes its classical models, but grave, chaste, noble,
skilful, and occasionally of a beauty which defies all
rivalry; which has the Syrian depth of feeling with
the European charm of form, and in which you seem
to hear the old sad Hebrew soul breathing itself
through the strings of an Italian lute." The first
complete edition of his Paraphrase of the Psalms
was brought out in 1566, and he dedicated it to Queen
Mary in the renowned epigram, " which," remarks the
same writer, " every Scotsman ought to have by heart."

> " O daughter of a hundred kings
>   That holdest 'neath thy happy sway
> This ancient realm of Caledon;
>   Whose worth outstrips thy destiny;
> Whose mind thy sex; whose grace thy peers;
> Whose virtues leave behind thy years—
> Behold in Roman garb I bring
> The work of Israel's prophet-King.
> Rude is my song as born afar
> From the Muse-haunted founts of Greece,
> Under the frigid Northern star;
> And but that aught that pleases thee
> Must ne'er displeasing seem to me;
> It had not looked on eyes save mine;
> Yet such a virtue flows from thine,
> Perchance my sorry child may own
> Some graces that are thine alone!"

CHAPTER IX

THE COURTIER

MR. HILL BURTON remarks that when Queen Mary, after the death of her husband, had to relinquish the throne of France and to content herself with that of Scotland, it was like leaving a palace for a cottage. The unbiassed reader, not to speak of the perfervid Scot, may detect a note of exaggeration in this statement, but, viewing it as a figurative speech rather than as a sober historical reflection, Buchanan's experience on landing in his native country after an absence of twenty-five years, mostly spent in sunny France, cannot have been very dissimilar to that of his Queen; for France was the land of thought and literature, and the contrast between the two countries in this respect was quite as great as between their climate and social condition. France was the home of that Humanism of which

Buchanan was now the head, and of all the countries of Western Europe, Scotland was perhaps the least affected by that great wave of literature and learning which was sweeping away mediæval thought and bringing in a new era of culture.

Various causes accounted for this. The Universities of Scotland, comparatively recent in their origin, were still very poor and ill-equipped. The aspiring scholar had as a consequence to seek his erudition elsewhere, and he as a rule migrated to Paris, which, on account of the "ancient league," offered him a cordial welcome. As a rule he remained there, or found his way to one or other of the continental Universities, where he would find congenial society, and where also his learning could be put to profitable use. Scotland then, as now, offered few prizes to the diligent student; the only promotion possible for him, and that at best was very uncertain, lay through the Church. The country, besides, was in a very unsettled condition; its constant struggle against England was not conducive to that calm which fosters the philosophic mind. The long minority of the young Queen, besides, gave occasion for incessant conflicts on the part of rival factions in Church and State; but the chief cause of the lack of concern in those Humanistic studies, which were prosecuted with so much zeal in neighbouring countries, was the interest in the reform of religion, which, in Scotland, absorbed for the time and for several generations afterwards, every other question. The religious and not the Humanistic movement was the one which dominated the minds of Scotsmen during the greater part of the sixteenth century.

It ought not, of course, to be imagined that there is any real antagonism between the heart and the head, between religion and culture. They are but two sides of the same shield, and conjointly form the highest type of manhood. It is only a narrow and onesided view of human life which would dissociate them, or place the one above the other. They are meant to go hand in hand, to act as mutual checks, and to be fellow-workers in the training and development of man's mind and spirit. It was fortunate for several of the countries of Western Europe, which have played a ruling part in modern progress, that the Humanistic movement preceded the religious. The ground was thus prepared for the sane hand-

9

ling of the new doctrines which Luther and the
other great Reformers launched upon the world.
It was fortunate also for England that the two
movements went hand in hand. This resulted in
a balance of power in Church, in State, and in
national life, which has characterised that country
ever since. In Scotland, on the other hand, the
Reformation preceded the Renaissance; indeed,
it may be questioned if the latter movement ever
took a real hold on the country, for with the exception of Drummond of Hawthornden, no writer of
distinction breathes the spirit of Humanism.

There are those, of course, who may see in this no
real loss, but a distinct gain; to them religion is
everything. We cannot agree with them. Religion
itself requires to be tempered by thought and
culture, or it may run into fanaticism. Besides, man
cannot live on religion alone, any more than he
can live on bread alone. He has other interests
which are perfectly lawful, and which in the name
of religion itself he is called upon to prosecute.
His reason, his imagination, and his fancy are
divine endowments which he dare not stultify or
starve. History calls for its narrator and inter-

preter, nature invites, nay demands, its investigator. The management of human affairs, national and civic, in their political and social relations, summons for its guidance the man of affairs. The work of the world has to be done, the life of man and of the universe has to be sung. These and a thousand other interests are as native to man and as divinely appointed as the worship of the sanctuary ; and true religion, in place of denying their divine right, recognises it and comes in to direct their course, to sanctify their labours, and to purify and bless their efforts.

We do not think that it is a mistake, or even an overstraining of historical facts, to state that the absorption of Scotland at this time in the religious movement to the exclusion of the other, accounts to a very large extent for the one-sided development which characterised the national life in the sixteenth and seventeenth centuries. During that long period the muse of poetry, which in the preceding century had sung its sweetest " with full-throated ease," was all but silent, and while England was rich in writers of the greatest genius, Scotland can hardly boast of one. We are of

course quite ready to admit the moral grit of
character which was rooted in the nation by its
wholehearted interest in religion; and that in after
generations, when, through the larger life and
opportunity of self-development which came through
union with England, the energies of Scotland found
fitting outlet, its earlier passion burst forth in
those activities and enterprises which have made it
great.

Buchanan, when he reached Scotland, some
time in 1561, while he would naturally miss
the cultured society to which he had been for
so many years accustomed, had developed new
interests which would make his loss more easily to
be borne. He had for some years been satisfying
himself, by careful study, as to the truth of those
questions which the Reformers had raised. If the
first period of his life be that of the Humanist, the
second is that of the Reformer, but of the Reformer
toned down and moderated by the culture which
he had gained by a careful and constant perusal of
the great masterpieces of antiquity. But his native
land was not, after all, so destitute of enlightenment
as might at first sight appear. In Church and

State there were men of learning, and of one of these Buchanan himself gives a very pleasing account.

During his visit to Scotland, while acting as tutor to the young Earl of Cassillis, he was on one occasion the guest of Gavin Dunbar, Archbishop of Glasgow, and, in a poem written to celebrate the event, he presents us with what Dr. Hume Brown very appropriately terms an "interior" in Scottish ecclesiastical society of that day, "such as the historians have not led us to expect." The table was generously but daintily furnished; there was no vulgar or vain display; the conversation was serious, but seasoned with Attic wit. The host led the discourse, and the guests, equal in number to the Muses, joined in with noble feeling and sympathy. The subject of conversation was the greatness and condescension of the Deity, and it was handled with sufficient knowledge and becoming reverence. This picture recalls the scene at Oxford, when Erasmus was the guest of Richard Charnock, Prior of St. Mary's College. The story of that famous symposium, which was taken part in by Colet and other distinguished English scholars, reveals the height of culture to which the learned men of that day had attained. Placed side by side with Buchanan's sketch of Gavin Dunbar's entertainment, it gives us an idea of the educated society which was to be found in the sixteenth century in both the Northern and the Southern Kingdom.

But the person in whose society Buchanan, on his return to Scotland, would seem to have found the greatest pleasure, was the Queen herself. She, from all accounts, had one of the brightest and most highly cultured intellects of the time. With the exception of Maitland of Lethington, the nobles who formed the Court were, for the most part, strong and hardy characters, who found their chief delight in battle, rather than in the playful interchange of wit which one associates with the society of the refined. Mary accordingly would welcome Buchanan. He was the representative not only of Scottish but of European learning. He was a king among men of letters, and his presence would add lustre to her Court. Nor was he a dull pedant immersed in his wealth of knowledge; he carried his learning lightly as a flower, and freely used it as the instrument of his strong thought and rich humour. He had on the Continent come into close and friendly contact with the noble and powerful, and his own gentle descent and acquired breeding, apart altogether from his great scholarship, would make him a fit companion for the highest in the land. His sharp tongue would give an edge to his intercourse with Mary, for she was noted for her hardy speech, and her severe and incisive estimate of her mother-in-law, Catherine of Medici, which did not smooth her future course, may be taken as an illustration of that sarcastic vein which characterised her.

The picture which Randolph, the English Resident, gives of the fair young Queen and the rough old scholar reading together after dinner in the ancient Palace of Holyrood "somewhat of Lyvie," is of another "interior," outstripping in interest that which Buchanan himself gives of Gavin Dunbar's entertainment in Glasgow. This was in the year of the Queen's arrival in Scotland, and until the murder of Darnley she and Buchanan lived on the most friendly footing. Mary's ambition was unbounded, and she would be nothing loath to have near her one of Buchanan's reputation, who could turn a Latin verse better than any man in

Europe, and celebrate the chief incidents in her life and the main events in her reign in such a way as to gain the attention and respect of surrounding nations. The man who stood at the head of the new movement which was revolutionising the world, was a powerful factor in the affairs of the nation in which for the time being he found his home. Erasmus was a force that had to be reckoned with by popes and kings and emperors, and the fact of Buchanan being recognised, employed, and even courted by Queen Mary and her nobles, is no matter of surprise, but must be accepted as a natural result of the conditions that then prevailed.

Buchanan, we know, during these years performed certain duties imposed upon him by State and Church, and in particular he seems to have discharged the functions of Court poet, or, as in our day we should say, of poet-laureate. He wrote Latin masques for the Court, on the return of Mary from France, on her marriage with Darnley, and on the baptism of her son James. He addressed epigrams to Mary herself, to the Regent Moray, and to two at least of the Queen's Maries, Mary Fleming and Mary Beaton. All these are light and playful in thought and expression. It is thus, for example, that he addresses Mary Fleming:

> " Receive what fruits the year affords in prime,
> O Fleming, flow'r and beauty of thy time ;
> Not to adorn thy head these gifts I send,
> No outward thing thy beauty can commend ;
> Only believe the Spring in best array
> Compared with thee is nothing but decay."

This epigram was evidently accompanied by a gift of flowers ; and in similar though less fortunate circumstances he addresses Mary Beaton :

> " Cold winter, flowers and fields oppress ; nowhere
> Can I find a nosegay for my lady rare,
> My muse, once fruitful garden, now by years
> Defaced is, and barren winter bears.
> Did comely Beaton's breath but once me touch,
> Spring, in her blossoms all, were nothing such."

While Buchanan was thus attending on the Court and serving it in the only way he could, he was still without any settled position or assured means of support. The greatest scholar of his country, he was still without any fixed appointment. Very few openings, perhaps, could present themselves, but the labourer is worthy of his hire, and such services as he could render, not to speak of the distinction which his presence gave, merited some fair if not very substantial recognition. The flunkey who opens the door and ushers the guests into the presence of a monarch receives his board and lodgings, silk stockings, buckled shoes, powdered wig, and a glorious suit of plush with gilt buttons and knee breeches; and is the scholar, who carries in his head the learning of the world, to wait patiently at the said monarch's gate with hat in hand and receive nothing? Is mere ignorant brute force with sword uplifted to be rewarded with countless acres and a peerage, and intellect sharpened to the finest edge by thought and study to be spurned aside as useless? It is to her credit that Queen Mary did not think so, for early in her reign she settled a pension of £250 Scots on Buchanan, and though this was a mere pittance it showed her good intention. The poet's hardy upbringing and modest wants would enable him to make the most of it.

Two years afterwards Buchanan's pension was increased, and made apparently more secure and permanent. Under a gift of Privy Seal he was made the recipient of a pension of £500 Scots from the lands of the Abbey of Crossraguel in Ayrshire, together with the whole tempor-

alities of the Abbey as well as the monastic buildings. This may seem a sufficient recognition of
Buchanan's services as poet-laureate, but it was in
reality a pittance compared with the rich spoils with
which the greedy nobles loaded themselves from the
possessions of the disestablished Church. Besides,
Buchanan was discharging other public duties which
certainly merited payment in cash. For in the
Register of the Privy Council, dated 6th February
1562-3, we read that he, along with another, had
been appointed to "interpret the writs produced in
process, written in the Spanish language forth of the
same, in French, Latin, or English, that the Queen's
grace and council might thereafter understand the
same."

To have a scholar like Buchanan within easy
reach for such and similar purposes was assuredly of
some importance and value, and his services were not
over-rated by the pension conferred on him. The
pension itself, however, turned out in the end to be
more a form than a reality. The Earl of Cassillis,
who believed that he had hereditary right to the
Abbey, was loath to relinquish his claim, and the
poor scholar had to appeal to the Lords of Council

to have his rights of possession vindicated. Other persons, making four in all, had vested interests in the Abbey lands, and Buchanan, finding his share to be a very doubtful asset, disposed of it on different occasions for annual payments that were merely nominal, and even these he had considerable difficulty in procuring.

Such facts, seemingly unimportant, become significant when viewed in relation to the charges that are made against Buchanan of ingratitude to the Queen, and of demeaning himself by sending to her and to certain of the nobility begging poems, which, neat and epigrammatic though they be, fail to do him credit. It is argued by those who see in Buchanan a monster of ingratitude and vindictiveness, that his pension ought to have shut his mouth ever after, and that in taking sides against the Queen he was guilty of a baseness that is altogether inexcusable. Reasoning of this kind is beside the mark. Was his tongue to be for ever tied because he received payment for work done? Was he to remain for ever loyal to a quondam friend and patron, though his reason and conscience called upon him to be loyal to truth? Was he to sacrifice his independence

of speech and action, and to refrain from vindicating
national right and justice because at one time he
was in favour with the Court, read Livy with his
Queen, and was rewarded for that and other State
services with the salary of a superior groom or
flunkey? To argue thus would be to stultify the
manhood not only of Buchanan, but of all who place
their duty to God and country above mere personal
feeling or friendly sympathy.

The same perverted view is taken by such as
see in Buchanan's begging epigrams a proof of moral
degeneracy. It is not, as it has been remarked,
rating their value too highly to say that a leading
publisher would in these days be only too glad to
give a hundred times more for such productions, if
written by a man of equal position, than what
Buchanan was likely to get for them from the persons
to whom they were addressed. Take this one, for
instance; the translation is excellent, but the original
is better. It is addressed to the Queen:

> "I give you what I have, I wish you what you lack;
> And weightier were my gift were fortune at my back.
> Perchance you think I jest? A like jest then I crave:
> Wish for me what I lack, and give me what you have."

Here is another to the Earl of Moray :

> " My gifts are late and slender, unto thee :
> In this, if any fault you think can be ;
> My fault not imitate, but soon amend,
> And lib'ral gifts unto your servant send."

These epigrams were evidently accompanied by a copy of verses, which, considering the writer, were of undoubted value.   Buchanan had not at his disposal the modern conveniences for the profitable sale of his literary wares.   The man of letters in the present day has at his elbow a publisher who is prepared to give him, should the author be a man of the first rank, as Buchanan was, a handsome sum down for his effusions, and afterwards a substantial royalty on every new edition.   The publisher advertises the book, puts it upon the market, and, as a rule, makes a fair gain for himself as well as for the writer.   No one ever dreams of abusing either the one or the other for their methods ; they are declared to be acting on sound business instincts and are commended for their enterprise.   No system of this kind was in vogue in Buchanan's day ; even Erasmus, who was the popular author of his time, and whose works passed through innumerable editions, was in a chronic state of impecuniosity. His begging letters form not an inconsiderable portion of his writings, and yet no one is too severe upon him on that account. These letters are among the most interesting that he ever wrote, they throw a considerable light on his character, and have taken their place as a part of the literature of the world.

The truth is, that such men, if they were to do the work which the world demanded of them, had to be supported by the generosity of the great. There were no openings for them such as exist in our day, in which they could enjoy a learned leisure. Their views debarred them from entering the Church, the only institution in which they could find protection and support; and even Buchanan's worst enemy could not wish that at the time of life which he had now reached, he should have continued the laborious task of regenting young lads in a Parisian College or wandering over the Continent as tutor to the son of a French Marshal. He was surely worthy of something better than that, and the post which he now filled in connection with the Scottish Court seems on every ground to have been a not unfitting one.

It ought, besides, to be remembered that the Crown

and nobility had in those days the almost entire possession of, and full control over, the wealth of the country. The Church, which a few years previously had shared the power, was now disestablished, and its endowments were grabbed by the greedy and grasping aristocracy. Whither, then, could a man like Buchanan turn even for the modest income which was necessary for his support? He had been roughing it all his life, and no self-respecting nation could allow a man of his rare talents, unique position, and sterling character to starve. He belonged to Europe as well as to Scotland, and for his native country to have denied him an honourable sustenance would have been a lasting disgrace. His only resources, meanwhile, were the Queen, the Earl of Moray, and the other leading personages in the land, who had a duty to perform to him and his like which they could not shirk without dishonour. The old feudal relations still held good. If the vassal fought the battles of his chief, the chief recognised his obligation to support and defend the vassal. If Buchanan by his pen brought glory to his country, his country was bound to maintain him and to make provision for his wants. Mary understood this quite well, and

the pity of it is that the poet was driven to the
necessity of reminding her and others of their duty.

" He had done a good work," as Mr. Robert
Wallace well remarks, " on the High Street of the
World. He had sung a song or played a melody
such as it would hear nowhere else. Was he not
entitled to send round his hat among the listeners?
Is it not what is done, *inter alia*, by every Parliamentary lawyer who goes into the House of Commons
to grind his axe, when the fitting occasion arises, and
he says to his party leader, I have fought two general
elections for you; I have spoken for you un-
numbered times in the House and on the platform;
I have voted for you up hill and down dale, through
thick and thin, right or wrong, and now I will
trouble you for that Chancellorship or that Chief-
Justiceship, or that Attorney-Generalship, or that
Puisne or County Court Judgeship that has just
fallen vacant? Except that Buchanan and his
work were not shams but realities, the cases are
the same. ' *Contemptis opibus*—despising wealth,'
is how Joseph Scaliger describes Buchanan. All
that he wanted was enough to maintain his independence and to do his work."

10

One of the best and, viewed in the light of subsequent events, not the least significant of all the poems written by Buchanan at this time, was his Ode on the birth of James the Sixth. It shows, for one thing, that his relations with the Court up to this time were of the most friendly order, but according to his chief biographer it gives an indication of the breach that was impending, and of the strong attitude which the writer was shortly to take up against the Queen.

Buchanan was not unfavourable to the Darnley marriage; he was not so keen a religious partisan as Knox, who saw in Mary's choice, because he was a Roman Catholic, the probable undoing of all that he and his fellow-reformers had accomplished. Darnley, besides, was the eldest son of the Duke of Lennox, and Buchanan, just like Knox himself in the case of Bothwell, may have been partial to the young nobleman because of old feudal relations. In any case, he was always friendly disposed to Darnley, wrote poems to him of a highly laudatory character, of which some critics make too much, forgetting the nature of the sentiment, often merely polite and artificial, which not infrequently characterised such effusions. If in the birthday ode which the poet addressed to " Henry King of Scots " he says, " On thee the kingdom's safety lies," he really means that on true government, of which the monarch is the head, the peace and prosperity of the country depends. Adulation, in these circumstances, is but the holding up of an ideal, which it ought to be the aim and duty of the King to realise.

In this birthday ode the poet looks into the future, and sees in vision the fulfilment of those dreams of national concord and progress which had for years been filling the minds and hearts of all true patriots. The chief result would be the union of the two crowns of Scotland and England.

> .   .   .   " And thou Britannia, beat
> So oft by foreign tempests, and so oft
> By thine own weapons almost quite destroy'd,
> Lift gladden'd now thy head, thy hopes confirm'd ;
> With boughs of peaceful olive bind thy hair,
> Repair thy dwellings, blackened with flames,
> And trim, foul with neglect, the dwellers fled :
> Dismiss thy boding fears, thy troublous cares,
> The stars now promise thee eternal peace."

He then addresses the parents, and counsels them as to the upbringing of the Prince. Upon their example and instruction his future and that of his country will depend.

> .   .   .   "So on the King
> The people fix their eyes, and him alone
> Admire, love, imitate, and by this glass
> Endeavour, as it were, to form themselves
> And all their manners."

It is not by harsh measures, but by love, that a monarch gains true sovereignty. If he desires his subjects to be pure and simple in their habits, loyal and devoted in their work, he himself must set the example. Then the poet turns round and utters the threat or warning, which according to some gives an indication of his doubts regarding Mary and of his own future conduct. If the King should prove unfaithful to his high trust, demean himself, or be by others dishonoured, his subjects are called upon to take speedy vengeance.

> "Nought better surely Nature hath conferr'd
> Upon the human race, nor greater will,
> Than a devout and temperate Prince, in whom
> The true and living image of God shines.
> That whether he himself by shameless vice
> Contaminate, or others violate
> By sword or treachery, God will exact
> Severest punishment in his wicked blood,
> Nor leave his spurned likeness unavenged."

This prophecy was to receive, sooner than Buchanan anticipated, a terrible and tragic fulfilment, and Queen Mary's court, like King Arthur's before it, was to be broken up and laid in ruins by the moral failure of her who was its head.

CHAPTER X

IT is customary when speaking of Buchanan to claim him as a Reformer as well as a Humanist. On looking closely into the matter, however, it will be found that his zeal for the Protestant religion does not entitle him to rank with those who were the prime movers in remodelling the doctrine and constitution of the Church. It is quite true, as he himself tells us, that when he returned to Scotland, he gave in his adhesion to the Scottish Church, and continued for the remainder of his life to be one of its most staunch and loyal members ; but his relation towards it was that of a silent supporter and quiet worker rather than a militant leader. He was evidently quite ready to undertake those duties for which he was specially suited and into which he could put his heart, and wisely refrained from taking

up a position for which he had no real enthusiasm.
We are accordingly not surprised to find him silent
with regard to the great doctrinal and other controversies which divided the nation, while taking his
share of the more practical activities of the Church,
for which by nature and training he was so well
adapted.

We first find him a member of the Assembly
which met on the 25th December 1563, and he
would seem to have acted in the same capacity
during subsequent years, until 1567, when he was
appointed Moderator. It may strike some as
strange that a layman like Buchanan should have
been elevated to the highest position in the Church;
but the Scottish Reformers did not regard the order
of ordination as essential even for the ministry of
the Word, much less for a position such as that of
Moderator of the Assembly, which simply demanded
the ruling of debate and the guiding of business.
John Erskine of Dun, another layman, was Superin-
tendent of Angus; and Queen Mary, when pressed
to hear one of the Protestant preachers, expressed a
preference for him because of his gentle and peace-
able disposition.

It showed the confidence which the Church had in Buchanan, that in its early struggles, when endeavouring to get its constitution into working order, it put him on most of the important Committees that had to deal with the new questions and unlooked-for complications which the circumstances naturally called forth. We have the record of the work of these Committees, and the results of their deliberations, and there can be no doubt that Buchanan's knowledge and common sense were of great help in finding a solution of the difficult and delicate questions with which they had, from time to time, to deal. The compliment which the Maréchal de Brissac and his officers paid Buchanan, in calling him in to advise as to the high military problems upon which they were deliberating, was repeated in very different circumstances, when Knox and his colleagues invited him to their counsels and asked him to take his part in settling those practical difficulties which the Scottish Church, in its first days, had to face.

It is easy, of course, to accuse Buchanan of lukewarmness. Highfliers will see in him only a Moderate, whose head may have been convinced without his heart being touched; or perchance at best an ecclesiastic whose soul delighted in Committees, and the petty work and secret wirepulling of which they are popularly believed to be guilty. It is not at all unlikely that a process of degeneration in this respect has been going on since Reformation times, and it would accordingly be utterly wrong to judge of the doings of Buchanan in the light of what takes place in our day. Nor should it be forgotten that he had reached his fifty-fifth year before he threw in his lot with the Reformers. That, assuredly, is not an age at which a man is expected to display the enthusiasm of youth. Besides, his conversion to the new faith was a long and gradual process.

The first indication of his interest in the Protestant Religion was in 1526, when he was a student in Paris, where he informs us he fell into the spreading flame of the Lutheran sect. Again, when he was in Scotland in 1535, he made his first serious attack, in his *Franciscanus*, on monkery and all its ways. This satire, to his astonishment, subjected him to so bitter a persecution that he had to flee the country. This, he further tells us, made him " more keenly hostile to the licentiousness of the clergy, and less

indisposed to the Lutheran cause than before."
But it was not until the last five years of his
residence on the Continent that he gave himself to
a critical study of the Scriptures, and to a serious
consideration of the " controversies that were agitat-
ing the majority of men." It was at that time, and
after this long process of thought and reflection, that
he finally formed definite opinions for himself, and
was fully persuaded in his own mind of the claims
of the Protestant Religion.

One cannot blame Buchanan for holding, silently,
perhaps, that they did not " know everything down
in Judee." His culture was not one-sided, like that
of the majority of the Reformers. The greater
part of his life had been devoted to a study of
the masterpieces of classical antiquity. He was
thoroughly familiar with the world of thought and
life which they opened up ; indeed, he was so imbued
with their spirit that he reproduced in his own
works the very body of past times. He was thus
necessarily devoid of that religious and theological
fervour which governed such men as Luther and
Knox. Constitutionally, perhaps, he was not inclined
to doctrinal discussions ; at any rate, he preferred to

follow the more secular calling of the scholar, and to take a place in the Protestant Church suited to his disposition, and much less lofty than that occupied by the Reformers.

Buchanan was the offspring of that Humanism which welcomed the Reformation as an ally in emancipating the spirit of man from the thraldom of an external authority. The world which the Renaissance opened up to the human mind was a new world. The natural man was seen for the first time for a thousand years, living and moving and having his being. He was presented to the aston-ished and enraptured gaze of the Humanists, aspiring after, worshipping, and even creating forms of beauty and ideals of life which to them were a revelation. The free spirit, which is every one's birthright, leapt from the pages of the Greek and Roman writers and speedily found entrance into the minds of the wondering scholars and filled them with a new life. Hence Buchanan views the Reformation in the light of Liberty. He sees in it an instrument for the crushing of the ecclesiastical authority which had for centuries bound the free spirit of man. He welcomed it as an awakening of the human intellect and as a reassertion of private judgment and individual right.

The Reformers, from their very position, had to assume a different attitude towards that spirit which they had called up from the depths of the past. They had to seize it and put it again into chains. Having disowned the authority of the Pope and the power of the Roman Church, they felt under the necessity of putting in their place some other force for the governance and the regulation of man's moral and spiritual life. Men like Buchanan may have thought that the divine ideal again discovered might have been sufficient, without forging any external bonds; and that the tyranny of the Roman Church would have been a warning against any attempt to perpetuate its evils, though in a new form. Such a position was a quite justifiable one for a man like Buchanan to take up. He probably did not require any sanction for his beliefs or any guide for his conduct, other than the Spirit of God as revealed in nature, history, Scripture, and his own conscience and heart; but he was the exception, and for the majority of the members of the Church an external authority was necessary.

Scripture, in the first instance, was the new authority which the Reformers set up. They made it the touchstone of doctrine, of worship, and of government. It took the place of the decrees and councils of the old Church, and dethroned the Pope from his time-honoured position as the head of the Christian world. The individual, ostensibly at least, was granted the right of private judgment; he was invited to read the Bible for himself, and to learn its saving truths. The Word of God, on which the Church itself rested, was surely the only source from which religious light could shine. All this sounds very well, but apart from the fact that other fountains of truth, such as nature and reason, should be taken account of in the building up of one's faith, the Reformers had but a narrow, and, in the light of present-day knowledge, an uncritical view of Scripture; their conception of its inspiration, for example, and its historical growth, cannot stand modern inquiry and research. In their hands the Bible threatened to become as great a tyrant as the Pope himself.

After Scripture came the Confessions. They sprang up in every Church with a rapidity that must have surprised even their framers. They were prepared, on the ground that the young Church must have definite authority on which it could take its stand. The necessity of this was perfectly clear. Outward symbols had to be devised, doctrinal statements had to be drawn up, rules and regulations for worship and government had to be laid down. No Church, as an organisation, could exist without them. Scripture with regard to such matters was too vague ; in any case, its instructions were too detached ; they must be gathered together, tabulated, and put into a logical and compact form. Thus did Confessions arise, and in the end they took away the right of private judgment, and that individual interpretation of Scripture which were the early boast of the Protestant Church.

It will not, therefore, be difficult for anyone to understand why it was that Buchanan did not feel inclined to become a minister of the Reformed Church, or to take a leading part in framing its doctrinal belief. He could at any time, during the first period of his life, have taken orders in the Church of Rome, and probably risen to a high position. At any rate, he could have saved himself from persecution, received sufficient for his temporal wants, and found that seclusion and leisure which would have enabled him to prosecute his favourite studies in peace. But he would not sacrifice his mental and spiritual independence; he would not place himself under an authority that would take away his liberty. He certainly did attack the licentiousness of the monks and ridiculed the doctrine of transubstantiation, but there is no evidence to show that up to his final breach with Rome he denied the main tenets of the Catholic Church. Humanism was a cry for liberty, so Buchanan determined not to put his spirit in chains. It must have been for the same reason that he declined to take any ministerial office in the Reformed Church. Like Erasmus, he refused to identify himself too closely with the doctrinal positions of either Church. Like some men in our own day, of wide culture and deep religious spirit, he looked beyond all the Churches, and saw a "new heaven and a new earth wherein dwelt righteousness."

It is easy, of course, to blame Buchanan for not joining the ranks of the stalwarts. Erasmus was much attacked by both sides for following a middle

course of his own.   What he desired was to see the
old Church reformed of its errors in creed and
government, and, failing this, he declined to defend
it.   For the same reason no power could induce
him to enter the Lutheran fold; he had no love
for the brand-new Church which the great German
set up.   He kept himself free, as far as he could, of
any external authority in matters of faith.   That
autonomy of the spirit which he believed was every
man's birthright he determined, as far as possible,
to keep inviolate.   Buchanan was evidently of the
same way of thinking.   Truth he loved, but truth
he believed ceased to be inspiring when it had to
be accepted, so to speak, at the point of the bayonet.
The only authority in religious matters which he
was prepared to obey was the Divine voice speaking
to him through his conscience and his heart.   Knox
was evidently quite prepared to work with Buchanan
under the conditions which the latter tacitly laid
down.   For as late as 1556 he wrote of them thus:
"That noteable man, Mr. George Buchanan, remains
to this day, in the year of God 1556 years, to the
great glory of God, to the great honour of the
nation, and to the comfort of those that delight in

letters and virtue." Knox's characterisation of him is significant. He holds him up to admiration as a unique and glorious type of the Christian scholar. This, indeed, is all that Buchanan pretended to be, and it says much for the Reformer that he had the good sense to see and appreciate in his friend qualities which the zealots of the new faith were strongly tempted to ignore, if not to despise. It was this doctrinal aloofness that enabled him also to live on friendly terms with the Queen. In his inward soul he belonged to no party ; what he aspired after was religious and civil liberty.

Sir James Melville of Halhill confirms, in his garrulous *Memoirs*, this impression of Buchanan's religious faith. " He was," says Sir James, " of gud religion for a poet." This, at first sight, sounds very faint praise. Poets, however, it may be remembered, have in the main been heretics ; their religion has seldom squared with the ecclesiastical beliefs of their time. Indeed, as a rule they discounted these beliefs, and contented themselves with forms of faith which were not often accepted by the common people. This does not prove that their religion was defective, probably it was nearer to absolute truth than what

11

was popularly held to be divine. Sir James's estimate, accordingly, signifies that Buchanan conformed
in his religion to the accepted standards, more than
most poets, but that he did not rise to the full
height of the enthusiastic Calvinists who accepted
the doctrines of the Church without demur. There
is not among all his writings any that may be
regarded as formally theological. The nearest
approach to a confession of his faith is his dirge
on the death of Calvin; but it is poetry, and it
attempts to blend the old heathen mythology with
the Protestant faith. Like all such attempts it
cannot be regarded as successful. The theological
views which it contains would have astonished no
one more than Calvin himself.

The truth is, Buchanan was essentially a poet, and
no surprise should be felt at the marked absence in
his writings of any allusion to, or direct statement
of, the leading doctrines of the Reformed faith. He
is silent regarding predestination, justification,
election, atonement, and the resurrection. He was
a critic and a humorist, and not a theologian. His
convictions, accordingly, however sincere and well
grounded, were not fired by that enthusiasm which

compelled Luther and Knox to do and to dare. Every man must be taken in his order, and judged accordingly; Buchanan's order was not that of the Reformer and Theologian, but of the Scholar and Humanist.

CHAPTER XI

RELIGION was not the only interest of the new times which had dawned on Scotland. Education, which, as we have already seen, was of deep concern to the leaders of public life, now began to be of more importance than ever. It was found to be the chief enemy of superstition, and to be the best means for developing the life of the nation and for preparing the citizen for the various duties demanded of him by the Commonwealth. Experts in this department may not have been so numerous or so well equipped as they are in our day; but, after all, the organisation of education depends for its success, not so much on the one-sided views of specialists as on the broad-minded conception of enlightened and patriotic statesmen. The age of the Reformation was singularly fortunate in the latter respect, and the educational future of Scotland could not have been placed in safer hands that those of John Knox. The scheme which he and his colleagues drew up for the reform of the schools and Universities of their native country is still, in its main features, the dream of present-day educationists, and an ideal which has received the approval of successive generations of Scotsmen, but which, alas, is still unrealised.

It was inevitable that those who were responsible for laying down the lines which should guide the future of Scottish education should call to their counsels a man of such varied knowledge and experience as Buchanan. He was the most distinguished scholar in the country, and he had been engaged nearly all his life in the instruction of youth. He had taught in some of the greatest schools and colleges on the Continent, and had gained a reputation which placed him as an educationist in the first rank. There is no evidence that he had any share in drawing up the Book of Discipline, in which Knox's scheme is adumbrated. Indeed, he was not in the country at the time; but in every subsequent attempt that was made, up till his death, to place the seminaries of learning on a proper footing and to regulate the nature of the instruction to be given, he took a leading part. His proposals met the same fate as those of Knox and Melville. They were never carried out, but that was not his fault; the reason was the same as that which has stultified the efforts of more recent times. The lack of funds, which cramps present-day movements in the direction of educational expansion, rendered his scheme and those of his able coadjutors nugatory; the only difference being, that while the modern millionaire refuses to give, the ancient nobleman took, that which in the national interest ought to be freely bestowed on the instruction of youth and the furtherance of the intellectual life of the people.

It was in 1566 that Buchanan received his first appointment, and for it he was indebted to the Earl of Moray. In that year he was made Principal of St. Leonard's College in the University of St. Andrews. The power of election to this post lay in the hands of the prior of St. Andrews, and as Moray happened to hold this office at the time, he fixed on Buchanan, with whom he was on friendly

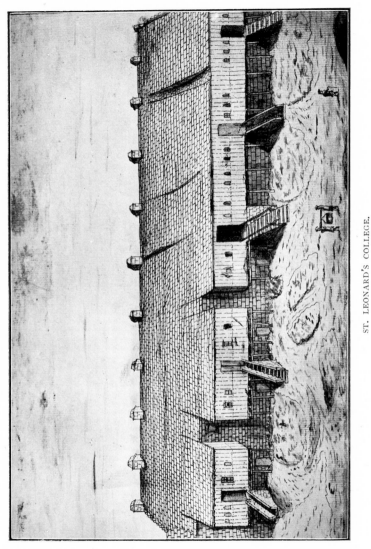

ST. LEONARD'S COLLEGE.

(*From an old Print in St. Andrews University Library.*)

relations.   The University of St. Andrews consisted
of three Colleges—St. Salvator's, St. Leonard's, and
St. Mary's.   The first was founded by Bishop
Kennedy in 1450, the second by John Hepburn,
Prior of the Abbey, in 1512, and the third, which
was begun by Archbishop Beaton in 1532, was
completed by Archbishop Hamilton in 1552.   St.
Leonard's, with which Buchanan was to be closely
connected for the next four years, was originally
founded for the accommodation of Pilgrims who came
to witness the miracles wrought by the bones of
Scotland's patron Saint.   It was a monkish institution, and was intended to foster superstition; and
even when it was transformed into a College by
Prior Hepburn, its object remained practically the
same.   The intention of the pious founders was
soon, however, to be thwarted.   It was the first of
the three Colleges to welcome the Reformation;
and to "drink of St. Leonard's well," became a
synonym for a belief in the Protestant faith.   In
another respect also its fortunes changed; it began
as the poorest of the three Colleges, but it soon
became the wealthiest.   At its start it was known
as *the College of poor clerks*, but the wise manage-

ment of its affairs by its governors, and the energy
and ability of its teachers, raised its position
financially and educationally, and drew to it a
greater proportion of the nobility and gentry than
repaired to its two rivals. This transformation in
its fortunes would not, we presume, be so strongly
resented by its pious founders as the other.

As the University of St. Andrews, like that of
Glasgow, was modelled on those of Paris and
Bologna, it is unnecessary to deal with its constitution or curriculum in detail, for in speaking of
Buchanan's life as a Student and Regent in the
University of Paris, we said on this subject all that
may be deemed sufficient. The Universities of
mediæval Europe, however similar they might be
in their origin and scope, differed of course from
each other in various ways; the nature and extent
of the instruction given were to a large extent
conditioned by their endowments, and as the University of St. Andrews, although the wealthiest in
Scotland, was still very poor, its educational equipment
was necessarily meagre. It suffered also from the
fame of its continental rivals, particularly the
University of Paris, which drew to it a large number

of young Scots, who then as now were animated by a wandering spirit; but the cause which reduced it, by the middle of the sixteenth century, to an almost helpless position, was the religious and civil troubles of the time. It was practically untouched by the Humanism which leavened the life of even the University of Paris, and found a home in the great schools of Oxford and Cambridge. The time was clearly ripe for the reform of national education as well as national religion, and the men who heralded in the new age set themselves to this task also with their wonted energy.

Three different schemes were drawn up during Buchanan's own lifetime for the reform of Scottish Universities. The first, as has already been indicated, was the well-known plan of Knox incorporated in the Book of Discipline. It formed a part of the general proposal of the Reformers for dealing with national education. Elementary schools were to be planted in every parish, secondary schools in the chief towns, and the course of study in the three Universities was to be so ordered that the best results possible might be attained. Knox in this, as in other matters, made use of the knowledge which he had gained on the

Continent. The proposals of the Book of Discipline
with regard to the University of St. Andrews were
as follows: The three Colleges of which it was
composed were to remain distinct, so far as the
subjects taught in each were concerned; but the
course of study was to be so arranged that the one
should lead up to the other. The first College was
to be devoted to the subjects which might be ranged
under the general title of Philosophy, the second
was to concern itself with Law, and the third with
Divinity. It may be noticed that in this arrange-
ment no place is given to Classics, as the secondary
schools were supposed to give sufficient instruction
in the ancient Languages. It may also be noted
that the University as thus determined would really
be a seminary for the higher education; it would
differentiate itself from the mediæval Universities
not only by its exclusion of the Classics, but also by
its insistence on the students being thoroughly
grounded before matriculating. We see in this
something both to commend and to regret. The
exclusion of the Classics indicated that the culture
of the Renaissance had found little or no recognition
in Scotland, and the one-sided development of the

national life which the Reformers favoured was
having results that would in the end prove detri-
mental to the symmetrical development of the people.
Approval, however, must be given to the attempt,
which is only now being realised, to make the
Universities seats of learning in the highest sense,
and not mere secondary schools. But the scheme
fell through. The rapacity of the nobles who
seized the property of the Church robbed the
Reformers of the means by which they hoped to
carry through those plans, which now remain as a
lasting monument of the enlightened and patriotic
views of their compilers.

The second scheme is the one with which
Buchanan's name is more closely associated. In
1563 a Parliamentary Commission was appointed
to revise the finances and to reconstitute the teaching of the Universities, particularly that of St.
Andrews. Moray, Maitland, and Buchanan were
the most important members of this Commission.
There is no record of the report which was handed
in, but the plan which was drawn up to meet the
wants of St. Andrews University has been preserved,
and it is generally supposed that it was mainly the

work of Buchanan. In the very first proposal there
is a confession of the failure of Knox's scheme, for
one of the Colleges is to be confined entirely to the
discharge of the functions of a secondary school,
and thus to serve as preparatory to the other two.
The second College was to give instruction in
Philosophy and Medicine, and the third was to be
devoted to Divinity. If the meagre equipment provided for the instruction of the last subject be any
indication of Buchanan's interest in Theology, that
interest must have been extremely weak, for the
staff was to consist of a single individual, who was
to be Principal and Professor all in one, and he was
to divide his time equally between Theology and
Law. The Classics, on the other hand, were to
receive full justice : they were to be taught through
six successive classes, and in the three highest instruction in Greek was to be given. No doubt
Buchanan was governed by the circumstances of the
hour. We cannot imagine that this was his ideal
of what a University should be. He had to make
the most of the situation, which was anything but
favourable to the higher education. That situation
has indeed taken a very long time to improve, for

University Reformers would seem to be as sorely bestead by hostile fortune now as then.

Some sixteen years afterwards another Commission was appointed, of which Buchanan and Andrew Melville were members. The new body was authorised to consider the Foundations in the University, and not only " to remove superstition and displace unqualified persons, but also to change the form of study and the number of Professors ; to join or divide the faculties ; to annex each faculty to such College as they thought most proper for it ; and in general to establish such order in the University as should tend most to the glory of God, profit of the Commonwealth, and the good upbringing of the youth in science needful for the continuance of the true religion." That this Commission was necessary may be seen from the remarks of James Melville, who declares that " after the zeal of the Reformation, regents and scholars cared nothing for divinity and for languages, arts, and philosophy. They had nothing at all but a few books of Aristotle, which they learned pertinaciously to battle and fight upon, without right understanding or use there-of." This Commission reported in

1579, the same year in which it was appointed, and the scheme which it prepared and which was ratified by Parliament, was the work chiefly, it is supposed, of Andrew Melville.

The recommendations of the Commission are such as we might expect; they bear evident testimony to the forceful and ardent spirit of Melville; they also reflect his special interests. The two Colleges of St. Leonard's and St. Salvator's were to be devoted to those subjects which at that time were included in the Arts curriculum, while St. Mary's was to be reserved for the teaching of Theology. It would seem that the whole strength of the University was to be concentrated on this subject, as St. Mary's was to have five professors, and the course was to extend over a period of four years. The study of Hebrew and cognate languages was to be prosecuted with energy. The Septuagint and other ancient versions were to be diligently studied, and the critical apparatus thus acquired was to be applied to the text and contents of the Scriptures. The whole time of four out of the five professors was to be devoted to this work, while the fifth was to give lectures on Systematic Divinity. Long vacations were to cease; time was precious; and it was ordained that for the future the students should have only one month's holiday in the year, that of September.

We have in this scheme a forecast of our own time, in one respect at least. The higher criticism is foreshadowed in the thorough knowledge that was demanded of the students of the original languages of Scripture, and in the stringent way in which this knowledge was to be applied to the elucidation of its meaning. That only one professor should have been set aside for the teaching of Systematic Theology, shows that there was not that supreme importance attached to dogma with which we credit that age. There is one glaring omission in the course: Church History has no place in it. It may have been thought that ignorance of the long story of the Roman Catholic Church would be a virtue; in fact, the Reformers did not regard it as a true Church at all. The History of the Apostolic Age would be fully dealt with by one of the four professors, whose subject would include the Acts of the Apostles; and the Professor of Divinity would no doubt be bound to lecture on the Lutheran and

Reformed Churches: so that the omission is not so marked after all. In any case, the course in Divinity, compared with anything that went before or has come after it, was to be thorough. It was to extend over eleven months out of the twelve, and the staff was to consist of five professors. At the present day the course extends to only five months out of the twelve, and there are but four professors. No science has within the last century progressed at a more rapid pace than Theology, and yet the Scottish Churches and Universities have done less than nothing to meet the wants of the new time; indeed, so far as theological equipment is concerned, they have, compared with the scheme of Melville, gone back in place of going forward.

Dr. M'Crie and Dr. Hume Brown differ in their estimate of the two schemes of Melville and Buchanan. They naturally champion the proposals of the man whose biography they have written. It may be sufficient, however, to point out that the special features of each scheme are such as we would naturally expect. Buchanan emphasised the Classical, and Melville the Theological side of the University course. Each followed his own predilection;

but compared with Knox's scheme they must be regarded as inferior and defective. The proposals of the Book of Discipline were broad-minded and progressive. The special parts relating to the Universities were the crown of the educational scheme that was to apply to the country as a whole. Knox, and those associated with him, dealt with the subject in a more detached manner than either Buchanan or Melville, and their policy, even in relation to the Universities themselves, was so ordered that every branch of knowledge and science, as then known, received its due share of consideration. It is not at all unlikely that in the near future another Parliamentary Commission may be appointed to deal with the educational institutions of the country ; and if one can judge, from the signs of the times, the proposals of Knox will in their fundamental aspects afford a guide in the framing of any scheme that will be drawn up. Many new features will undoubtedly have to be added, but the co-ordination of elementary, secondary, and the higher education will, if we are not much mistaken, be one result ; and the reorganisation of the various Colleges in the country, with their respective faculties,

12

and the relation of the whole to the Universities, must form an integral part of the scheme.

We have very little information about Buchanan's life while he acted as Principal of St. Leonard's. We know from the records of the University what his duties must have been. He would "superintend the domestic economy of the College, attend to the religious exercises of its members, and on Wednesdays and Fridays he would instruct the Presbyters, Regents, and all others who chose to attend, in sacred and speculative theology." On entering upon his duties he found his College very poorly attended, but within a year the numbers began to increase, and before he left it was the most popular of all the three Colleges, containing more students than the other two put together. His great name would undoubtedly be the attraction. His personal qualities, in addition to his fame and scholarship, must have added to his popularity as a teacher. He would seem to have always maintained the most cordial relations with his pupils, and to have gained not only their respect but affection.

One who studied under him bears this testimony

to his power of interesting and attracting youth.
"Buchanan," he says, "was of such flexibility of
mind that with boys he became a boy; he had
alike the faculty and the will to adapt himself to
every time of life, yet always in such a way as
never to forfeit the respect due to himself." Nor
did he lose sight of his pupils; he encouraged
them, and by personal effort he endeavoured to
push their fortunes. An interesting letter of his
remains, in which he urges his friend Beza to
assist Jerome Groslot, a young student whose
father had shown him great kindness when he was
in France, and for the same youth he pens a
testimonial, a model of its kind, which, coming
from such a man as Buchanan, was sufficient to
have secured preferment for any promising lad.
Another, Alexander Cockburn, one of the "bairns"
who had been under Knox's tutorial care, and who
passed away in early manhood before his scholarship had time to ripen, forms the subject of two
poems by Buchanan, in which he expresses admiration for his talents, and regret at his untimely
death.

He also took upon himself, along with two others,

the humble task of preparing a Latin Grammar for the education of Scottish youth, and manifested his interest in the intellectual welfare of his native West by presenting a number of Classical Works to the University of Glasgow. That clannishness, which is alleged to be a trait in the Scottish character, no doubt possessed Buchanan notwithstanding his wide culture. He never forgot that he was a Lennox man; and though he had never been a student at the University of Glasgow, he would feel that it had local claims upon him which he could not resist. It is accordingly generally believed that the favour which Queen Mary showed to this University was due to him, and what is known as the *erectio regia*, which is associated with the Regency of Morton, was due to the influence of "our dear Privy Councellor George Buchanan, Pensioner of Crossraguel, and Keeper of the Privy Seal." It is thus that his name is appended to the deed of gift.

CHAPTER XII

WE now enter upon a new phase of Buchanan's life. Shortly after his appointment by the Earl of Moray to the Principalship of St. Leonard's College, St. Andrews, events took place which plunged the country into civil war. On the 9th of February 1567, Darnley was murdered, and on the 15th of the following May the Queen was married to the Earl of Bothwell. The great controversy which these sudden and startling incidents gave rise to, has continued with almost unabated and uninterrupted interest to the present day. Every year sees a fresh contribution to the discussion, and finality on the subject would seem to be as far off as ever. The cause of this undying concern, in what everyone admits to have been a foul murder and a very questionable marriage, is undoubtedly Queen Mary herself. Had she, as someone has remarked, been ugly, or even plain, men would have ceased troubling themselves over much about her long ago; but she is reputed to have been beautiful, and is known to have been fascinating. She was young, clever, and charming; every man felt the power of her spell, and all, with the exception of Knox, seem to have fallen under it; even Buchanan himself, with the susceptibilities of a poet, had a genuine admiration, during the early days of their friendship, for his Royal mistress. The charm still continues, and sober historians, when discussing the tragic events of those far-off days, have a feeling of tenderness for the fair fiend, or victim, as the case may be, and hold a flirtation with her across the space of three centuries. Had Mary, with all her ability, beauty, and grace, passed her years in peace, and gone down into the grave at a good and honoured old age, that sentimental interest in her and her doings which still continues would very probably have never existed. But it is just the aberration in her moral conduct which is involved in her marriage to Bothwell, and the murder of Darnley, that keeps her memory so fresh. Supreme wickedness, if it be the result of an affair of the heart, appeals by a strange perversity to human nature, much more strongly than supreme goodness; at all events, it displays the war of passions, and gives material for those reflections on man's complex nature which, however trite, never seem to pall.

The country was naturally divided over the question which these startling events raised. There was no doubt in the public mind as to who was the real murderer of Darnley. Every sign pointed to Bothwell, and the Queen's delay in giving facilities for bringing him to trial, the mockery of the trial itself when it did take place, and her indecent haste in marrying the murderer of her husband, confirmed the suspicion that she herself had a hand in the dastardly deed, and roused the resentment of the nation against her. The change in the public feeling towards Mary was as strong as it was sudden. There can be no denying her popularity, up to her marriage with Darnley. Her people were proud of her, and, under the guiding hand of Moray, public affairs were managed on the whole with prudence and

skill.   Her hasty union with Darnley was her first
great mistake; he turned out to be a young fool,
and growing disgusted with him she fell into the
hands of the unscrupulous adventurer who would
not seem to have cared much for her, but was
willing enough to use her for the realisation of
his own vaulting ambition.   Mary was evidently
possessed by a passion for Bothwell which blinded
her to every consequence.   She even declared, in
her wild frenzy, that she would rather go through
the world in a white petticoat with him, than
without him reign over Scotland and England
and some other countries besides.   Even after her
final separation from him at Carberry Hill, she
declared to Lethington that her one wish was to
sail with Bothwell away from these shores; and
the wily secretary dryly remarked that he thought
she could not do better.

Plain people who have never felt the grand
passion, or who are ignorant of human, and
especially woman's, nature, seem to think such
extravagance of emotion absurd and impossible.
But all one has to do is to look out on contemporary life, or to read the public prints, to find

almost daily examples of what we are now considering. Mary was a Stuart and a Tudor and a Guise all in one. With such an ancestry as she had, and such an upbringing in the Court of France, her life and fate, while they may shock, should not altogether surprise us. The facts of human nature give sufficient warrant for the facts of Mary's career, and, however much we may pity the tragic ending of a life and reign that began with so fair a promise, we must bow before truth and believe the unfolding tale of History.

From what we already know of Buchanan it would be easy to forecast the course which he would take; he declared against Mary. We do not, so far, find any trace in his life of compromising with what he believed to be falsehood or error in doctrine or in conduct, and it was not at all likely that, if he believed Mary to be guilty, he would hide his convictions and act towards her as if nothing had happened. The Queen, unfortunately, had become impossible. If she had, even at the last moment, agreed to repudiate Bothwell and to govern constitutionally, all might have been well, but she struck out at the nobility who

had separated her from her husband, threatened
them with death whenever she regained her liberty,
and made it clear that her own will, or passion
rather, would be the sole guide of her public and
private conduct.   Her deposition thus became, in
the interests of the nation, a necessity.   Additional
proof was soon forthcoming of her complicity in
Darnley's murder.   The *Casket Letters*, which have
played so important a part in this strange history,
were about to make their appearance.   Those who
believed in their genuineness, and among them was
Buchanan, had now no doubt of her guilt.   He, at
any rate, was convinced.   He believed that she was
an adulteress and a murderess; and the action
which he subsequently took, in proving this to the
civilised world, has earned for him the undying
hatred of all the defenders of Mary from his own
day till ours.

The *Detectio*, the work in which Buchanan
arraigned Mary before the bar of Europe, is, of all
his writings, the one which has been the most
severely attacked, and by it, according to some,
he must stand or fall.   As a piece of rhetoric, in
which every sentence adds to the weight of the

argument and hurries on the passion of invective
to its inevitable climax, it has been compared to
similar classic masterpieces of antiquity. It is
possible that Buchanan may have had such examples
in his mind. He felt that he was the champion
of a great cause. The world had been startled by
the tragic events which convulsed Scotland, and the
friends of constitutional government had some
doubt of the legality and righteousness of the
Scottish nation in dealing thus with their Queen.
Buchanan stood forth as the vindicator of his
country, and in his philippic he determined to
prove that Mary was impossible as Queen of Scots,
and that the only course which any patriot could
pursue was that which had been followed in de-
posing her.

The work was written in Latin, and being the
production of a scholar of European reputation, it
at once commanded the attention of the civilised
world. It was soon thereafter translated into
French, English, and Scotch, and being written in
a popular style it was widely read by the common
people. There can be no doubt that Buchanan's
Detectio not only influenced the Courts of France

and England against Mary, but to a large extent also inflamed the passion of the Scottish people against their Queen. A great responsibility rested on him. This he must have known ; and it is hard to believe that he could have written as he did, without being persuaded in his own mind that he was recording fact.

It is not at all surprising that the defenders of Mary should have singled out this work of Buchanan's for attack. It has been their aim to discount and to discredit it. They have denied its facts without, however, rejecting its conclusions. Nor has the author himself escaped ; indeed, he has on account of this work been the subject of scathing and countless epithets. Both he and his pamphlet have been held up to obloquy. One or two specimens of the way in which some critics speak both of him and it, may not be unwelcome. They will show, at any rate, that the power of invective is not all on one side. "Buchanan," says a modern Mariolater, "was without doubt the most venal and unscrupulous of men." "The Latin poet," says another, "the Latin Historian who sang of and libelled his Queen, his pupil." "He was old,"

continues the same writer, " a Lennox man, and an
advanced Liberal." " The luckless nymph to whom
his Psalms were dedicated, he was afterwards to
assail with all the ferocity of senile spite and all
the weapons of unscrupulous calumny." The *Detectio*
itself is characterised as " Buchanan's famous libel " ;
" atrocious libel " ; as " grossly inaccurate and amus-
ingly inconsistent " ; " the highly coloured narrative
of Buchanan." Both the writer and his book are
summed up as " grotesque adventures, invented,
or at least adapted, by Buchanan, whose viru-
lent animosities were utterly unscrupulous, and
whose clumsy invective was as bitter as it was
pedantic."

Our readers will not take it amiss if we refuse
to be tempted, even by such strong and bitter
statements, to enter upon a defence of Buchanan
which would drag us through the length and breadth,
the height and depth, of the great Marian controversy. Books innumerable deal with the subject,
many of them more defaced by passion than adorned
by argument. Those who believe in the guilt of
Mary, manifest no joy in proving their conclusions ;
they come, as a rule, to them with reluctance, and

manifest a noble pity for the brave and brilliant creature who sacrificed her fame and fortune, as many of her sex before and after her have done, for one altogether unworthy. It may be regretted that they who, believing in her innocence, defend her, are not able to speak of her accusers in language equally temperate, but ruin their cause with vituperation and spleen. But the remarkable fact stands out, that even the most recent champions of Mary, while they condemn Buchanan's *Detectio* for its bitterness, and reject many of its details, practically admit its conclusions, and hold the Queen to be guilty of the very crimes for which he, on behalf of the nation, charged her before the world. Even the *Casket Letters*, the most damning evidence of Mary's guilt, have, after the most searching criticism on the part of native and continental scholars, been practically accepted as genuine. It was these letters that brought conviction to the minds of those who were responsible for the conduct of affairs, and which led up to the deposition of Mary. They had evidently great weight with Buchanan; and, firmly believing that they were written by the Queen, he felt justified in undertaking and discharging the

task which was imposed upon him, of vindicating
the national honour in the eyes of the world.

The worst that can be said against Buchanan's
Detectio is, that it does not display that calm and
judicious spirit in the selection of evidence and in
tone of expression which should characterise such
a work. But the point is: What was the object
of Buchanan's *brochure*? It was not intended as a
judicial statement of the case, which should be put
before a court of law; it was written with the
express purpose of appealing to the intelligence of
the people, both of his own and neighbouring
countries. The nobility, who made themselves responsible for the new government, prepared in their
"Book of Articles" such a statement against Mary
as the legal mind could appreciate. Buchanan's task
was different, and for the object in view it must be
admitted that he achieved a brilliant success. The
narrative is direct and spirited. The incriminating
evidence is historically and briefly stated, and every
fresh proof of guilt against the Queen leads up to
the final catastrophe. It is possible that Buchanan
did not sufficiently sift his evidence; he may have
lent too ready an ear to the gossip of Court and

street.   He thus gave a handle to his critics which
they have not failed to seize; but the special
pleading which they have to resort to, in order to
disprove his main contention, reveals the weakness
of their case.   Grant that its spirit is bitter,—but
how, it may be asked, could it be otherwise?   What
a disappointment and shame had their young Queen
proved to herself and to the nation?   What a scandal
had she brought upon her people, who were noted
for their national pride?   What a shock must her
conduct have been to men whose conscience had
been quickened by the preaching of the Reformed
faith?   Individual and national righteousness had
been outraged; and the man who in his youth had
in his *Franciscanus* scathingly satirised the Roman
priesthood, now in his advancing old age felt compelled, in his *Detectio*, to vindicate the nation in
its condemnation of the Queen.

One of the gravest charges which the critics of
Buchanan bring against him is that of ingratitude.
They declare that he spurned the hand that fed
him, and cursed the generous soul that blessed
him.   This, we must admit, is a new light in which
to regard Buchanan.   If his conduct up to this

point, even in the eyes of his severest censors, be
practically without reproach, it is passing strange
that he should all of a sudden, and at a time of
life when his character ought to have been formed,
have displayed such moral turpitude. But how
stands the matter? He received, it is true, as has
been already noticed, an annual pension of £500
Scots, or £25 sterling, from the Queen—that and
nothing more; and this pension, derived from the
temporalities of the Abbey of Crossraguel, was
very irregularly paid. Was this royal bounty—
a mere pittance to what was showered on that
"vile knave Davie"—to shut the mouth of the
moralist and satirist for ever? Did it imply that
he had sold his conscience and his honour? Those
who censure Buchanan in such unmeasured terms
should face these and like questions, and answer
them not in the light of sentiment, but of reason
and truth.

The poet, it ought to be remembered, more
than earned what he received, and the independent
attitude which he maintained towards Mary, even
in the days of their most friendly intercourse,
showed that he had not bartered his soul for

13

courtly favour or sunk his individuality in sycophancy to the Queen. He, for instance, made no secret of his adherence to the Reformed faith. He was a regular member of the General Assembly, the one institution in the country that Mary chiefly detested, and he was Moderator in 1567, the very year when the Assembly gravely debated the question of her guilt. Buchanan, it is clear, preserved, even in relation to Mary, that autonomy of spirit which characterised him all through, and he would feel under no obligation to remain silent or inactive when the time came for striking a blow in defence of his country's honour. The *Detectio* may be very unpleasant reading for Mary's defenders, but it is only perverted criticism which can accuse Buchanan of ingratitude for writing it.

Nor should we overlook, in dealing with this subject, the poet's numerous and unbroken friendships. Some of these have already been enumerated, others will be subsequently mentioned. No Scotsman of his time had a wider circle of friends. The greatest scholars in Europe were among them. Many of these friendships he formed in early years, and they remained unbroken while life lasted.

There is no record of his ever having been a party to any of those quarrels of authors which were not uncommon even in his time. He never gave indications of mean jealousy, nor was he himself an object of envy; if he had rivals, he disarmed their hostility by his generous praise. So unaffected was he by his literary success that he never manifested any signs of arrogance, or had occasion to resent disloyalty on the part of a friend. His conduct towards Mary must then, on the showing of his critics, be regarded as the great exception, which, it must be admitted, they have not a little difficulty in accounting for. It is much easier, we contend, to regard it in the light of Buchanan's character as a whole, and to see in it not a proof of ingratitude, but the action of one who, in obedience to his conscience and in the interests of righteousness and truth, preferred the good name and honour of his country to any past admiration he may have had for his Queen.

Another charge is brought against Buchanan. He is accused of having been a toady and self-seeker. The early poems which he wrote to Mary are brought forward in proof. Here, again, we are met with a great exception. *Contemptis opibus*—despising wealth—is, as we have seen, the way in which Joseph Scaliger describes him, and the poet's career all through showed that he despised not only wealth, but also place and power. Even fame, so dear to the rhyming tribe, would seem to have had little attraction for him. He was a "Stoic philosopher," says Sir James Melville, and if Stoicism consists in indifference to riches, to honours, and to applause, the description is accurate enough. At no period in his career did he possess, or even strive desperately to obtain, those temporal blessings which the vast majority of men would seem to regard as the very essence of life. He was the frugal scholar to the very last. It is unnecessary to labour this point. The man who for over fifty years had made learning and not money his chief aim, and who had made many sacrifices and endured much hardship to maintain his independence, was not likely to turn sycophant and a time-server all at once. It is surely all the more impossible to believe this when the only proof adduced is that he wrote pretty and complimentary verses to his young and beautiful Queen. We have no doubt that his critics have attempted something of the same kind themselves; if not to the Queen of the realm, then to the queen of their heart; their only regret being, that they failed where Buchanan succeeded. Buchanan, indeed, would have been singularly remiss in his duty if, as the poet of his age, he had not written complimentary and even flattering verses in honour of Mary. It was the fashion of the times, besides. Kings, queens, and great personages were addressed in terms which indicated not so much what the writer believed them to be, as what he hoped they might be. An ideal was set before them which they were asked to aspire to. It is in this light Buchanan's verses should be regarded; and thus judged, their writer, so far as this phase of his relations to Mary is concerned, has very little to fear.

It is in the light of his age also that his *Detectio* itself should be judged. It was an age in which nothing was done by halves. In war as in love, men were bold and fierce, and in controversy they seldom veiled their feelings, but spoke out in a manner which might be intolerable in the times in which we live. The very title of the *Detectio*, as

given in the Scots translation, is sufficiently startling.
"Ane Detectioun of the Duinges of Marie, Quene
of Scottes, touchand the murder of hir husband,
and hir conspiracie, adulterie, and pretensed mariage
with the Erle Bothwell; and ane Defence of the
trew Lordis mainteineris of the Kingis gracis,
actioun, and authoritie."

Dr. Hume Brown, in referring to this point, says:
"It would be utterly uncritical to judge this performance by present canons of taste and good
feeling. The *Detectio*, like all Buchanan's literary
work, must be judged by the standard it is necessary
to apply to all the productions of Humanism," and
he gives a quotation from Mr. R. C. Christie's
life of Etienne Dolet to mark the traditions of
Humanism in its mode of conducting controversy.
"It is impossible," remarks Mr. Christie, "to defend,
and difficult to excuse, the scurrility with which
Dolet speaks of the greatest scholar and the fore-
most man of letters of his age (Erasmus). All
that can be said in extenuation is that scurrility
of this kind was a common practice of the literary
men of the day in writing of their opponents; that
we find it in men distinguished for their learning,

ability, and virtue; and that, violent as the language of Dolet appears, it is far less violent, far less scurrilous, and far less unseemly than that which Julius Cæsar Scaliger used of the same great man, or that which Luther applied to Henry VIII. and his other opponents, while it is absolutely moderate in comparison with the language of Filelfo, of Poggio, and of Valla."

But we need not after all go back to the Middle Ages for specimens of invective that far outweigh in violence anything ever penned by Buchanan: all that we have to do is to refresh our memory with the epithets which modern critics fling at him. Some of these we have quoted; but of one thing we may be certain, that if he were alive, most, if not all, of the choice expressions in which his enemies characterise him and his work, would never have been written. In their case, at any rate, the old proverb, with a slight variation, is undoubtedly true: " A living dog is more to be feared than a dead lion."

Buchanan was one of the Commissioners who in 1568 accompanied the Earl of Moray to York, and afterwards to London, for the purpose of placing the

indictment against Mary before Elizabeth. The
writing of the *Detectio* was his share of the work.
While in London he would seem to have had
pleasant social intercourse with Elizabeth's great
Minister, Cecil, and his wife, to both of whom he
wrote verses. He had friendly relations also with
Roger Ascham, Elizabeth's classical tutor, and,
according to the habits of the times, they exchanged
complimentary verses.

On returning to Scotland, in the beginning of
1569, Buchanan resumed his duties as Principal of
St. Leonard's. The country, however, was in a very
unsettled state, and his work must have been con-
siderably interrupted by the conflict of parties.
The two factions that were for some years to plunge
the nation into civil war were gathering strength,
and the strife between them was, if short, to be
sharp and bitter. The King's party and the Queen's
party divided the country, and Buchanan, who had
committed himself to that side which championed
the cause of national freedom and constitutional
government, worked in the interests of the young
King, and employed his pen in his service. He
accordingly wrote two political pamphlets, "The

Admonitioun to the trew Lordis" and the "Chamæleon," the only works that were written by him
in the vernacular.

The first was really an attack on the Hamiltons,
who thought that they saw in the present crisis a
chance of securing the throne for the head of their
house. They were playing fast and loose with
both parties, and were ready to take advantage of
any turn in the game that might be favourable to
their own cause. It was one of their number who
had killed the Earl of Moray, and they were the
hereditary foes of the house of Lennox, the head
of Buchanan's own clan. Buchanan, accordingly,
warns the Protestant Lords to beware of the
Hamiltons, whose history as political firebrands he
traces. The two parties of the King and Queen
might be regarded as patriotic, but the Hamiltons
were self-seekers, to whom the good of the nation
was as nothing compared to their own.

The second piece was an attack on Maitland of
Lethington. Its title, the "Chamæleon," suggests
the changeable nature of the Secretary's character
and policy. He was a turncoat without moral
backbone. In those times of dead earnestness

he was a light mocker who played the game
more for mischief than from any set purpose.
He had perhaps the cleverest brain of his day, in
Scotland at least; but no one could depend upon him,
and at the moment when Buchanan wrote his satire
he was stealthily but steadily plotting for the Queen.
The writer sketches the ever-changing career of
Lethington, and holds him up to ridicule as an
unreliable statesman of whom any party might well
be quit. The Secretary heard of this production,
and, knowing how a satire by Buchanan would
expose him to the scorn of Europe, he made
every effort, even to raiding the printer's premises,
to prevent its publication. His efforts were not
without success; the "Chamæleon" was not printed
till 1710, although copies of it were in circulation
shortly after it was written.

Critics differ in their estimate of these two pieces.
As they are Buchanan's sole venture as a writer of
the Scots dialect, they are of value. They show
the stage which the vernacular had reached as an
instrument of literary expression, and Buchanan's
own power of handling it. What first strikes one
is the manner in which he forms his sentences. He

was evidently framing his style on classical models, and while this helped him towards clearness it prevented him from managing the language in that independent and masterful way which characterises the writings of Knox. Buchanan had not only done all his writing in Latin, but most of his thinking as well, and when he came to write in the vernacular his work was more a translation than an original production. All the same, that power of thought and command over his ideas, which in the end condition style, enabled him to write the vernacular with clearness and force.

CHAPTER XIII

THE TUTOR

IT was no fault of Buchanan's that James the Sixth turned out to be the wisest fool in Christendom. Whatever wisdom he had may justly, in part at least, be attributed to Buchanan, while his folly was all his own. It is as tutor to the young King that Buchanan is chiefly associated in the minds of his countrymen. He was appointed to this post by the Privy Council in 1570 when James was only four years of age, and he continued to act as the young monarch's master and mentor for the next eight years. Queen Mary was now a prisoner in England and the Regent Moray was assassinated. The loss of such a man was a serious blow to the Government and a great grief to Buchanan. But those in whose hands was the management of public affairs were determined to resist to the death the

return of the Queen, and to carry on the government,
in the name of the young King, in a constitutional
manner.

It was accordingly of the highest importance that
James should not only be well educated, but be carefully and wisely trained for his future position and
duties. These promised to be of the loftiest nature,
for he would in all probability be king not only
of Scotland, but of England and Ireland as well.
He was to be the greatest King, so far as the extent
of his dominions were concerned, that these Isles
had ever seen. It says much for the governors of
the nation that they saw and realised their responsi-
bilities. James was given into the safe keeping of
the Earl of Mar at Stirling Castle, and a number
of capable men, of whom Buchanan was the chief,
were appointed to train him. Four young nobles
were selected as companions for the King and to
receive instruction with him. Buchanan gave up
his Principalship of St. Leonard's and entered upon
his new duties with a deep sense of their importance.
His selection reflects credit on the Privy Council,
for he was not only a great scholar but an enlightened publicist, who had ideas on the relations of a

king to his people which were far in advance of
the times. It was these very ideas that the Scottish
people were trying to enforce by means of the
Revolution through which they were passing. They
only partially succeeded ; another and a greater
Revolution had to take place before Buchanan's
ideas were to be fully realised.

The Privy Council were well aware of Buchanan's
opinions, and they probably hoped that along with
the Latin and Greek which he would be sure to
teach James, he would also implant in his mind true
conceptions of government. Their hopes were to be
disappointed. Buchanan discharged his trust and
taught the young monarch the way in which he
ought to govern a free people ; but James was a
Stuart, and a blind believer in that divine right of
kings which first brought his mother, and then his
son, to the scaffold. Buchanan was assisted in his
tutorial work by Peter Young, who steadily kept an
eye on his future. This placeman carefully avoided
offending the King, and he received in consequence,
and in due time, a Knighthood and a pension.
Buchanan was of a different spirit. So far as his
own advantage was concerned, he looked neither

before nor after, and he discharged his duties in so strict and unbending a way as to kindle the after resentment of his pupil, who, while proud of having had such an instructor, condemned his works and would have destroyed his person. Sir James Melville gives the following account of Buchanan's relation to his pupil, throwing at the same time a side light on Mr. Peter Young's attitude. "My Lady Mar was wise and sharp, and held the King in great awe, and so did Mr. George Buchanan. Mr. Peter Young was more gentle, and was loath to offend the King at any time, carrying himself warily as a man who had a mind to his own weal by keeping of his Majesty's favour, but Mr. George was a Stoick philosopher who looked not far before him. A man of notable endowments for his learning and knowledge of Latin poesie, much honoured in other countries, pleasant in conversation, rehearsing at all occasions moralities short and instructive, whereof he had abundance, inventing where he wanted."

It is interesting to learn the extent and character of the studies to which the young King had to apply himself. Mr. Peter Young, whatever other good thing he may have done in the world, has left a record of the tasks which were prescribed for his royal pupil. After morning prayers he read Greek, the New Testament, Isocrates, or Plutarch; he was also exercised in the rules of Grammar. After breakfast he read Cicero, Livy, Justin, or modern history; in the afternoon he applied himself to composition, and, when time permitted, to arithmetic or cosmography, which included geography or logic and rhetoric. This, it must be admitted, was a pretty extensive and thorough scheme of study for a scholar of eight or ten. The method of cramming which we associate with our own day was evidently not unknown in the times of which we are speaking. It ought to be noted, however, that those physical exercises which are held to be so necessary for the development of the modern youth were not neglected, for two relatives of the Earl of Mar, David and Adam Erskine, Commendators of Dryburgh and Cambuskenneth, were appointed to superintend his training in bodily exercises and accomplishments. James's education was meant to be all-round and thorough. Never did a royal youth get a better chance, and it says much for the nation that whatever notions the King himself may have afterwards

QUEEN MARY AND JAMES VI.
(*From Lesley's History.*)

entertained, it at least had lofty conceptions of what a Monarch ought to be in mind, body, and character.

Buchanan has always received full credit for the remarkable scholarship which James displayed, but even he did not regard mere book-learning as the highest accomplishment for a monarch. Like all wise men, he laid the chief stress on right ideas and character. In a poem addressed to Randolph, the English Resident, he states his ideal of a prince. "You often urge me to paint for you what manner of King I should wish, were God to grant one according to my prayer. Here, then, is the portrait you want. In chief I would have him a lover of true piety, deeming himself the veritable image of highest God. He must love peace, yet be ever ready for war. To the vanquished he must be merciful, and when he lays down his arms he must lay aside his hate. I should wish him to be neither a niggard nor a spendthrift, for each I must think works equal harm to his people. He must believe that the King exists for his country and not for himself, and that he is in truth the common father of the State. When expediency demands that he

14

shall punish with a stern hand, let it appear that he has no pleasure in his own severity. He will ever be lenient if it is consistent with the welfare of his people. His life must be the pattern for every citizen, his countenance the terror of evil-doers, the delight of those that do well. His mind he must cultivate with sedulous care, his body as reason demands. Good sense and good taste must keep in check luxurious excess."

This was no empty ideal that Buchanan cherished; he did his best to have it realised in the character of his pupil. We have sufficient proof of this in the remarkable Prefaces in which he dedicated to the King three of his works, his *Baptistes*, his *De Jure Regni*, and his "History." In these productions we have Buchanan's views on government. In the first he strikes a blow for liberty, in the second he lays down the doctrine that a king exists for the people, and in the third he illustrates his opinions by examples taken from the history of his own nation. Nor did he think that he had done his duty by writing these works merely, he drives home their lessons in Prefaces which the King, young as he was, could not but understand. That James should in after

years have failed to profit by the teaching of his
master was his own fault, or the fault of those who
swelled his vanity by making him believe in his
divine right. Buchanan may have had a presenti-
ment of the manner in which the King, when he
became his own master, might regard the views
which he was endeavouring to enforce. That James
did afterwards resent them, and did his best through
Parliament and otherwise to have them condemned,
we know; indeed, it was only Buchanan's own death
that saved him from being tried at the instance of
his old pupil for sedition. It accordingly says all
the more for Buchanan that he neither "feared nor
flattered any flesh" however royal, but spoke the
truth, and strove to save the King and country from
that conflict which he saw was certain unless his own
views of a free and just government were endorsed
and practised. Buchanan's conduct as the King's
tutor is the best argument that can be used against
those who charge him with having been in his
relations towards Queen Mary a sycophant and
self-seeker. He could, if he had been of the same
moral build as "Mester Peter Young," have so in-
gratiated himself into the good favour of James as

to have secured emoluments and promotion that would have made his old age easy and comfortable. His reverence for truth, however, and his concern for his King and country compelled him to make every personal sacrifice. He had the reward which usually falls to those who live and work for the larger hope. He earned the ingratitude and resentment of him for whom he toiled, but Time, the true arbiter, has amply justified his conduct.

Anecdotes describing the relation between Buchanan and his pupil have been handed down to us. Even though they were not duly vouched for, they are so characteristic that one is inclined to accept them.

A quarrel sprang up one day in the class-room between two of Buchanan's pupils, the young King and the Master of Mar. The dispute was about a sparrow. The little bird belonged to Mar, and James coveted it. The owner declined to give up his property, and a scuffle ensued in which the poor little bird was killed. The affair was reported to Buchanan, who gave the young King a box on the ear, and told him that "he himself was a true bird of the bloody nest to which he belonged."

A study in composition was one day set to the royal pupil. The theme was the conspiracy of the Earl of Angus at Lauder Bridge during the reign of James the Third. This was the occasion on which the Earl gained for himself the nickname of Bell-the-Cat. After dinner, when the King and young Mar were amusing themselves, they made so great a noise as to disturb Buchanan at his studies. He requested the King to desist, but no attention was paid to his command. He then declared that unless he were obeyed he would enforce his orders with something more telling than words. On this the young Prince called out, But who will bell the cat? His master thereupon threw aside his book and so severely chastised him that his wailing attracted the Countess of Mar, who hastened to the scene of disgrace. She instantly demanded of Buchanan how he dared to lay his hand upon the Lord's anointed? Buchanan's reply is recorded, but being more expressive than polite we shall leave it to the reader's imagination.

One other anecdote may be mentioned. It is given on the authority of Buchanan's nephew. James in his early youth was much addicted to

favouritism ; indeed, all through life he was a victim
to this weakness. His master determined if possible
to correct his pupil's conduct, and adopted the
following expedient. "He presented the young
King with two papers, which he requested him to
sign, and James, after having slightly interrogated
him respecting their contents, readily affixed his
signature to each, without the precaution of even
a cursory perusal. One of them was a formal
transfer of the regal authority for the space of
fifteen days. Having quitted the royal presence,
one of the courtiers accosted him with his usual
salutation, but he announced himself in the new
character of a sovereign, and with that humour
for which he was distinguished began to assume
the demeanour of royalty. He afterwards preserved the same deportment towards the King himself, and when James expressed his amazement at
such extraordinary conduct, Buchanan reminded
him of his having resigned the crown. This reply
did not tend to lessen the monarch's surprise, and
he began to suspect his preceptor of derangement.
Buchanan then produced the instrument by which
he was formally invested, and with the authority

of a tutor proceeded to remind him of the absurdity of assenting to petitions in so rash a manner."

James was a precocious youth, and very quickly assimilated the instruction that was imparted to him. His early acquirements are borne witness to by two such capable observers as Killigrew, Elizabeth's Representative in Scotland, and by James Melville, Andrew's nephew. Killigrew visited the King at Stirling, and his tutors, with the laudable purpose of showing off their pupil's accomplishments and of duly impressing the mind of the English Resident, called upon James to make " pretty speeches " and to " translate a chapter of the Bible from Latin into French, and from French into English." This he did, much to the satisfaction of Killigrew. The young Prince was then asked to dance before the visitor; this he also did, " with a very good grace." James Melville, who accompanied his uncle to Stirling when the latter wished to consult Buchanan on some University matters, was evidently more impressed than Killigrew by James's ability and acquirements. The royal scholar, at the bidding of his tutors, made a display of his accomplishments similar to that which he

gave before Killigrew. Melville's opinion is on
record : " It was the sweetest sight," he says, " in
Europe that day, for strange and extraordinary gifts
of ingine, judgment, memory, and language." " I
heard him discourse," he adds, " walking up and
down in the auld Lady Mar's land, of knowledge
and ignorance to my great marvell and astonishment." Making every allowance for the fact that
this " sweetest sight " and infant prodigy was the
heir to the Scottish and English thrones, there
can be no doubt of James's remarkable facility in
acquiring knowledge. We are not surprised at the
great hopes which Buchanan entertained of his
future ; but facility in acquiring knowledge is one
thing, character and judgment are another, without
which all the knowledge in the world is as nothing.

There can be no doubt that James's very remarkable acquirements made an impression on his
countrymen, to begin with at least, and in particular
on his English Courtiers. A careful critic like
Mark Pattison admits that he " was the only
English Prince who carried to the throne knowledge
derived from reading or any considerable amount of
literature," and this opinion is confirmed by later

investigations. But, notwithstanding this admission, James's knowledge was superficial, and it only tended to make him a pedant instead of a wise man. His Scottish subjects had very little respect for him, and he was tolerated in England not on his own account, but chiefly because through him the country had escaped from the iron rule of the Tudors.

On certain occasions when it suited his purpose James spoke well of Buchanan, but his general attitude towards his preceptor's memory was hostile in the extreme. When at the Scholastic Conference, which was held before his Majesty at Stirling, an English Doctor who chanced to be present expressed his admiration at the King's command of the Latin tongue. "All the world," replied James, "knows that my master George Buchanan was a great master in the faculty. I follow his pronunciation both of the Latin and Greek, and am sorry that my people of England do not the like, for certainly their pronunciation utterly spoils the grace of these two learned languages. But you see all the University and learned men of Scotland express the true and native pronunciation of both."

The King's unfavourable opinion of Buchanan

was no doubt chiefly due to his master's views on civil government and his opinion of Queen Mary, the King's mother. The severe discipline to which Buchanan subjected James, while not originating would very probably add to his quondam pupil's inimical feelings towards him, for of a certain personage James in after years was wont to say that he "ever trembled at his approach, it minded him so of his pedagogue." This inclination to belittle Buchanan, and to destroy if possible his reputation, was encouraged by his Courtiers, who wished to gain his favour by feeding his vanity and condemning those whom he disliked. "I cannot fail to present to your Majesty," said no less a person than Lord Bacon, "the unworthiness of the History of England in the main continuance thereof, and the partiality and obliquity of that of Scotland in the latest and largest author that I have seen." Buchanan's reputation has survived the animosity of his royal pupil, and shines much brighter in the annals of History than that of James himself.

Buchanan has been charged with creating that character in James which his own and after ages have so severely condemned. It is suggested that if his master had been more patient and sympathetic with him, he might have fostered in the soul of his pupil those high ideals which he himself entertained. To this it may be answered that Buchanan had a very poor nature to deal with. Greatness of soul can be guided and developed, but not created by even the most painstaking and sympathetic of masters. Buchanan, we have seen, was popular with the young, and in one instance at least he had great credit with an old pupil; we refer to the son of the Maréchal de Brissac. In the Prefaces in which he dedicates several of his writings to the King we have evidence of the careful and even anxious manner in which he tried to inspire the mind of James with high ideals; and while his utterances are frank and pointed he regards his pupil in a kindly spirit, and even with admiration and hope. The truth is, James was not cast in a great mould; he was little by nature, and like all small-minded men he turned round in the end upon him who strove to impress upon him a high conception of his duties.

Buchanan held his post as tutor to the King until his death in 1582. For a number of years, however, he must have delegated his duties to Peter Young and others. Indeed in 1578, after the fall of Morton, James emerged from the stage of tutelage and shook himself free not only of his tutors but for a time of the Regent as well. Buchanan was appointed to other posts. The Regent Lennox made him Director of Chancery and afterwards Keeper of the Privy Seal. This office, which he held till 1578, gave him a seat in Parliament. He was also one of a Commission appointed to codify the civil and municipal laws. These various offices, while they did not make exorbitant demands on his time, invested him with considerable influence, and bore evidence of the respect and confidence of his countrymen.

CHAPTER XIV

BUCHANAN was essentially a man of letters, and it was more by circumstances than by temperament that he was drawn into the vortex of religious reform and politics. He acquitted himself with credit in the two last spheres of activity, as he did with distinction in the first, but his mental bent and early training pointed to his life's work as a scholar. We have seen the part he played as a Churchman, and we have now to consider his position and conduct as a politician.

Knox, and at a later date Andrew Melville, were both great public characters. They bulked in the eyes of the nation not only as churchmen but as politicians of the first rank. In other words, their influence upon the nation affected its secular as well as its religious interests, and they endeavoured to guide its general policy towards a definite end. Buchanan in his own sphere was greater than either of them, and it is as a man of letters that he stands or falls; but it says not a little for him that in the public duties which he undertook he displayed both talent and energy, and accomplished work of permanent value.

There can be no doubt that his position as tutor to the young King made him a man of importance in the eyes both of his own country and of foreign nations as well. His influence in forming the religious and political beliefs of James was felt to be very considerable, and he was approached by the lovers of the new faith and by the upholders of constitutional government to bring up the young prince as a Protestant and the representative of a limited monarchy. He endeavoured, as we have seen, to discharge his duty in both respects, and James's failure to respond to his teaching was not his fault. As tutor to the King and as one of a council of twelve for the direction of the Prince's conduct, he resisted the policy of Morton, who as Regent made every effort to gain possession of the person of the King. He also impressed the emissaries of Queen

Elizabeth as one of the eminent Scotsmen whose favour was worth securing. They classified him among the *Biencontents* of the third class, that is, persons who " were not commended by the Regent, yet by others thought meet to be entertained." We can well understand why Morton should not have recommended Buchanan to Cecil as one of those who might be useful in fostering friendly relations with England. Morton and he did not see eye to eye on various subjects, such as the policy that should be pursued with regard to the Church and the independence of the young King in relation to the Regent; but the opinion of those who were supposed to know, set some store on Buchanan's influence; and his services, if he were willing to render them, were valued at a pension of a hundred pounds by the English Court if he cared to accept of it. Whether he or any of the others to whom larger or smaller pensions were assigned, after the fashion of the times, ever received them, we cannot tell.

It is, however, not so much as an active politician as by his views on government that Buchanan takes a place among those who have influenced national affairs on a large scale. It is as an author that he, in this sphere, as in every other, comes prominently into view. In 1579 he published a work on civil government which caused a very considerable stir in his own day and for a century afterwards. Indeed, it gave rise to as keen and widespread a controversy as the *Detectio* itself. Buchanan, probably without intending it, turned the political world of his own day upside down, and the echo of the strife which his book produced is still heard in the air. The work we refer to is his well-known dialogue on the Rights of the Crown in Scotland, *De Jure Regni apud Scotos.*

From the Preface, in which he dedicates the book to King James, we learn the occasion on which it was written. He says that it was composed "at a time when the affairs of the nation were in a most turbulent condition," and that his intention in writing it was "to explain the reciprocal rights and privileges of Kings and their subjects." This must have been about the year 1570, or perhaps somewhat earlier, when Moray with his fellow-Commissioners returned from England. The policy which had been followed by those who took upon themselves the responsibility of government after the murder of Darnley, had been subjected to hostile criticism both at home and abroad, and just as in his *Detectio* Buchanan defended the action of the Protestant Lords in their treatment of Mary, so now in his *De Jure* he challenges the criticism of the whole world regarding their conduct in relation to those questions of constitutional government which had been raised. The book, he tells the King, had lain almost forgotten among his papers. He was wishful at the time to repress its publication on the ground of public concord, but having recently lighted on it he deemed its publication expedient, in the hope that it might contain " many precepts necessary to his tender age, and at the same time testify to his own zeal to his service, and admonish him of his duty to the community."

In his work Buchanan follows the Socratic method. He discusses the subject in the form of an imaginary dialogue between himself and Thomas Maitland of Lethington, the younger brother of Secretary Lethington, whom he satirised in the " Chamæleon." Young Maitland is represented as

15

newly arrived from France, and Buchanan is anxious
to hear news from the land which had been his
home for so many years, particularly the opinion
generally entertained of recent transactions either
by the French or by such strangers as he had met
in France. "For I was sufficiently aware," he continues, "that the novelty of the events, as is usually
the case, must have furnished occasion and materials
for universal discussion." Maitland replies that the
conduct of the Scots in the murder of Darnley and
in the subsequent treatment of Mary was freely
criticised and condemned. To this comes the reply
that murder must be punished, and if Mary was
found guilty of her husband's death, she, even
though a Queen, must be tried by the same laws
as would condemn the meanest of her subjects.

The argument of the dialogue may be briefly
stated. Buchanan holds that man is by nature a
social animal, and that the diseases of the body
politic require a physician, who is the King, and
whose duty it is to preserve the health of the State
or to restore it. But how does a King come into
existence? He is chosen by the people, is subject to
their will, and a body of laws is framed for his guid-

ance. He is placed in his exalted position to admin-
ister the laws and to mete out equal justice. It is
not the King who makes the laws, but the people.
He simply acts as interpreter. Tyrants are kings
who hold the power in defiance of the people, and
place themselves above the law. The Scottish kings
have always been subject to the will of the people,
who in several instances dethroned or banished
them. On being crowned, the Scottish kings swear
to preserve the laws of their country, by which their
authority is limited. When St. Paul enjoins obedience to the higher powers, he means the principle
of authority, and not individual rulers. A king, if
he transgresses the law, should be judged by it,
even though the penalty be death; if he defies the
law, he has broken his compact with the people,
who are within their right in slaying him.

These views, familiar as they are to us, descended
as a thunderbolt on the heads of absolute rulers
and the defenders of divine right in Buchanan's day.
They cannot be said to be new, for they find free
expression in the writings of classical antiquity, and
the Greek and Roman States frequently put them
into practice. But immediately previous to the

Reformation there would seem to have been an emulation among crowned heads as to which would rule most autocratically, and it was in the interest of this species of absolute government that Machiavelli wrote *The Prince*. This production, which called forth numerous rejoinders, simply raised the very question which it tried to settle. The principles which lay at the root of Humanism and the Reformation struck at civil right as well as mental and spiritual freedom. They brought up for discussion and settlement the citizen's relation to the State as well as man's relation to thought and to God.

But the questions which in the sixteenth century called for practical settlement had their antecedents far back in the past. Just as Luther and his fellow-Reformers had their precursors in Hus, Jerome of Prague, Wycliffe, and others, so Buchanan and those who along with him discussed the rights of the people in relation to their sovereigns, gave expression to ideas which had been subject to a long process of development. Professor Flint, in his masterly work on the *History of the Philosophy of History*, gives a full and luminous sketch of the evolution of the ideas of progress and of freedom,

from the earliest times until they began to be
embodied in those scientific works on history
with which the main body of his book deals. The
student of Buchanan, although he had no other
aid to guide him, could, from a reading of Dr.
Flint's work, trace the links in the chain which
connect the *De Jure* with the earliest reflections on
human life and liberty. Dr. Hume Brown, as one
would expect, takes up the same theme, especially
in its bearing on Buchanan's work, and gives a very
helpful sketch of the different writers who paved
the way for the civil Revolution of the sixteenth
century. Full justice is done to the Humanists
who, inspired by their classical models, contended
for those rights for which the best spirits of the
ancient world fought and died. The Christian
Church had also its share in the defence of human
right against absolutism, for it arrogated to itself
the right of excommunicating any ruler who defied
the authority, which it maintained was inherent in
it as God's vicegerent. It thus placed the kingdom
of heaven, as represented by itself, above any
earthly empire, and preached the doctrine that
kings must govern in accordance with the will of

God. During the Middle Ages many voices, such as those of Gregory of Tours, Isidore of Seville, John of Salisbury, Thomas Aquinas, Duns Scotus, and others, gave clear utterance to the same ideas, insisting on the freedom of the citizen, the subjection of the ruler to the will of the people, and the right of a nation to depose a tyrant and, if needs be, cause him to be slain.

It was not, however, till the Reformation that any serious attempt was made to have these ideas put into force. In Germany, owing to the States that were chiefly affected by the new doctrine supporting Luther, there was no real conflict between the people and the reigning prince. In France it was different, and Calvin had to draw up with extreme care that part of his *Institutes* which deals with the relation of the Christian citizen to the government of the country. Protestantism as defined by him, and accepted by the mass of its adherents, was a law-abiding religion; but in certain circumstances representative authorities were admitted to be entitled to defend, even at the risk of civil war, the rights of the people against a tyrannical prince.

It was in Scotland that these principles found
their first practical illustration, and to it is due the
credit of striking the first blow for that liberty
which heralded in the new age. The position of
Knox is familiar to most readers; the political
pamphlets which he wrote, immediately before his
final return to his own country, clearly reveal his
views on this important subject. Indeed, at an
earlier period, he had formed definite opinions on
the rights of the members of the Commonwealth,
and these were so far advanced that Calvin hesitated
to accept them. In his famous interview with
Queen Mary, when this very question was raised,
he boldly stated that if a Prince should overstep
the limits of his authority he should be forcibly
seized and kept under restraint until his mad frenzy
had left him; and further, should discipline fail to
bring him to a right state of mind, the nation would
be quite within its rights in depriving him of his
power.

Knox would no doubt be influenced by the spirit
of the age and by the special significance which the
Reformed Faith attached to human personality.
He must also have been brought into touch with

continental thinkers whose views on individual right and liberty were beginning to take definite shape. But there can be no question that the writer who directly influenced him was his old master John Major, whom Professor Masson characterises as the "first Scottish Radical," and who in his "History" laid it down that "as it was the people who first made kings, so the people can dethrone them when they misuse their privileges"; and again, "as it is for the benefit of the whole body that an unhealthy member is removed, so is it for the welfare of a State that a tyrant should be cut off." Major as a theologian was a Schoolman. He was practically uninfluenced by the Humanism which inspired Buchanan, but as a political thinker he evidently held views which anticipated and paved the way for the bolder doctrines of his successors. Buchanan's *De Jure* was not after all so startlingly fresh as might at first be imagined; the stir which it caused arose from the fact that what had previously been promulgated as a theory was now taking practical shape. It was no rose-water revolution that it advocated, but one of fire and blood.

That it did cause considerable commotion, almost

immediately after his publication, is seen from the eagerness with which it was welcomed by some, and the drastic measures for its suppression that were taken by others. One of his correspondents on the Continent, writes him to the effect, that so keen was the desire to see his book on the part of such men as Sturm, Hotman, and others, that it was borrowed the very moment of its arrival, and that he had since been unable to procure a reading of it. The attitude of the ruling powers in Buchanan's own country was very different. In 1584, two years after the author's death, the *De Jure* and the "History" were condemned by an Act of Parliament, and all copies were confiscated. Eighty years later, in 1664, and again in 1688, when the storm that had been brewing for a century was coming to a height, the Privy Council issued a proclamation prohibiting the circulation of manuscript translations of the *De Jure*, and in 1683 the University of Oxford did Buchanan the honour of publicly burning his political writings along with those of Milton and others. Dr. Irving gives a detailed and interesting sketch of the controversy that continued to be waged over Buchanan's famous dialogue.

The political commotion which it occasioned convulsed the country for two centuries. If it has now ceased to interest, it is because the positions for which it contended have become part and parcel of the constitution of the country.

There are different opinions regarding the intrinsic merits of Buchanan's work. Dr. Hume Brown, for instance, does not rank it very high as a scientific discussion of the important subject with which it deals. He places it in this respect on a much lower level than Bodin's *Republic* and even than the *Franco-Gallia* of Francis Hotman. These two works were in a sense epoch-making, and Professor Flint speaks of them with the warmest praise. But it ought to be remembered that Buchanan's tract was written for a special purpose. Its object was to justify the nation's conduct towards Mary, and to prove that the action which had been taken was in accordance with the constitution of the realm. He resented the criticism of foreign nations, and it is with a defiant note that the work begins and ends. Buchanan was not a philosopher nor a jurist in the scientific acceptation of the term, he was primarily a man of letters, and all his writings bear the impress of his bright and lucid mind. He did not discuss first causes, but was content to treat any subject which he handled as the cultured scholar and thinker. This tract is no exception, and its almost perfect form and style had not a little to do with its immediate and continued success. It was enough for Buchanan that he proved his thesis; and his Dialogue found its justification in inspiring Milton's famous *Defence of the People of England*, and in the subsequent fulfilment at every point of the political doctrines which it taught.

CHAPTER XV

BUCHANAN departed in one respect from the example of his classical models. He took upon himself the rôle of the historian as well as the poet. The great writers of the ancient world confined themselves, as a rule, either to prose or to poetry; indeed this is true of the most distinguished authors of all times, and it seems on the first blush a somewhat bold and hazardous undertaking for Buchanan to challenge the opinion of the world on his merits as a writer of prose as well as of verse. It cannot be said that he had already done so by his *Detectio* or his *De Jure*, for the first was a popular *brochure*, written for an immediate purpose, and the second had been cast aside and had lain all but forgotten among his papers. His *Rerum Scoticarum Historia* was deliberately conceived and elaborately worked out, and upon it, more perhaps than even on his *De Sphæra*, he believed that his fame would rest. His position as a poet was now an assured one, and it says much for his courage and confidence that he was prepared to risk his great literary reputation by the production of a historical work on a large scale.

It is evident that the first thought of the work did not originate with himself. In the Preface, in which he dedicates the book to the King, he gives an account of the manner in which the task was suggested to him. He says : " When, after a peregrination of twenty-four years I had at length returned to my native country, the first object of my care was to collect my papers dispersed by the malignity of former times and in many respects exposed to improper treatment. For partly by the undue partiality of my friends, by whom they were prematurely published, partly by the immoderate licence which printers, assuming the character of censors, exercise with respect to other men's works, I find many passages changed, chiefly according to their respective fancies, and some vilely corrupted.

" While I was attempting to remedy these inconveniences, the sudden entreaties of my friends disordered all my plans. For all of them, as if they had conspired with each other, exhorted me to relinquish those performances of a more trivial nature which rather soothe the ear than inform the mind, and to occupy myself in writing the history of our own nation. This occupation, they urged, was worthy of my age, and of the expectations concerning me which my countrymen had formed; and no other subject presented stronger incentives of praise, or promised to confer a more lasting reputation." He further justifies the undertaking on the ground of the importance of the subject, and by the fact that no one had hitherto done it full justice. He sees in it also what should be of inestimable value to James himself, for he considers it a shame that while the King was familiar with the history of other countries he should remain ignorant of that of his own. Besides, the great historical personages with whom he would have to deal would, from their respective conduct and character, afford the young monarch guidance in the conduct of public affairs; and, in fine, the work would somewhat atone for his own inability, owing chiefly to infirm health, to discharge his duties as tutor to the young Prince with the faithfulness that he had desired.

The last twenty years of his life were chiefly devoted to this work. He discharged many other duties, as we have seen, of both a personal and public nature, and not a little of his time would be taken up in the revision and publication of his collected works. In letters written during this period to Randolph and other friends, he bemoans his infirm health, and expresses a fear that he might not after all be able to finish the task which he had set himself. An unfortunate delay also took place, from some documents either not being available or having gone amissing, but with that indomitable perseverance which characterised him, he struggled on, and brought down his history to the death of the Regent Lennox in the year 1571. Sir James Melville finds in Buchanan's silence as to the Regency of the Earl of Morton an additional proof of the historian's hatred of the Earl. This, we contend, is very slight evidence from which to draw so definite a conclusion. Morton was not, even on Melville's own showing, the most pure minded and unworldly of men; on the contrary, he was admittedly avaricious and cruel. Indeed, it is possible that he imputes his own opinion to Buchanan, for the latter speaks of Morton without asperity, and discusses his actions in the most judicious manner. The truth probably is, that Buchanan's "History" ends with the Regency of Lennox, because the writer had neither time nor strength to continue it any farther. He was busy with the proof-sheets on his deathbed. In his case his work and his life ended together.

Buchanan was not the first who attempted to write the History of Scotland. He had precursors in Fordun, Boece, and Major, but he felt that full justice had not been done to the subject. This opinion was evidently shared by many others, and the thought that upon him rested the burden of putting a true face on Scottish affairs, from the earliest times to his own, would prove an incentive to produce a work that would show him at his best. Whatever opinion may be held of his "History," no one has hazarded the remark that in it Buchanan has fallen below himself. From beginning to end it is written with a vigour, a clearness, and a terseness that would be difficult to surpass. It is well proportioned, and graced by a diction which makes the narrative singularly attractive. It is written in Latin, and while this is unfortunate, in view of the present ignorance on the part of his countrymen of that language, it was fortunate at the time, for it made the whole of Europe familiar with Scottish history. Indeed, up till the beginning of the eighteenth century, it was widely read, but since then, owing to the decline in the knowledge of Latin, and to fresh Histories of a more scientific nature having appeared, it has been superseded. Of few books of a similar character can it be said that they have held the field for nearly two centuries. Those who disparage Buchanan's work might do well to bear this in mind.

It is rather singular that the first of the twenty books of which his " History " is composed, is the one which has been received with the warmest commendation. At all events, his latest formal biographer, regarding Buchanan's production in the light of the modern scientific conception of history, says that " this chapter is in some respects the most valuable of his whole work." It anticipates, though unconsciously on the writer's part, the idea of

16

climatic influence on the inhabitants of a nation.
He describes in detail, and from the careful observation of an eye-witness, the physical condition and
social habits of the people, especially those of the
western islands. The question of the origin of the
different races that compose the Scottish nation is
then taken up. He passes by as fiction many of
the legends which "Scottish vanity" had induced
some of his predecessors to accept as truth, and
gives copious and on the whole not inapt quotations
from ancient writers in support of his belief that
at the dawn of history the original inhabitants of
the whole island were Britons, Picts, and Scots.
Following Boece with a too confiding trust, he briefly
sketches the history of those legendary kings whose
existence had really no place except in the brain of
Scottish romancers. It is true that he prunes down
Boece's list somewhat, but he gives enough of it to
provoke the attack of Bishop Lloyd, who says,
not without humour, "Boece put these monks'
tales into the form of a History, and pieced them
out with a very good invention, that part in which
he chiefly excelled. Buchanan put them into excellent Latin ; he could have put them into as good

verse if he had pleased; and that had perhaps been better, for then they would have looked more like a poem."

Buchanan shows his superiority over his predecessors in his more critical account of the Roman occupation, and differs from them with regard to his estimate of the early religious history of Scotland. Reformer as he was, he could not but view with dislike the intention and teaching of St. Augustine, who introduced into the simple and Apostolic practices of the Church of St. Columba, the ritual of Rome. He brushes aside as a specimen of the "English lies," which it was one of the aims of his work to controvert, the supposition that Athelstane was king of the whole of Britain, thus holding Scotland in suzerainty. He fails to see the significance of the reign of Malcolm, and of the influence upon the Church and country which resulted from that monarch's marriage with Margaret, who had been brought up at the court of her great-uncle, Edward the Confessor, and who was followed into Scotland by many English emigrants. He has nothing but praise for David, and, while dating from his reign the dawn of Scottish literature, he agrees

with Major in regretting his impoverishment of the
Crown for the sake of the Church. His patriotism
rises to its full height in his account of the heroic
deeds and wise statesmanship of Wallace and Bruce.
The death of James the Second, with the dispute
that arose over the Regency, gives him an occasion
for stating his views regarding female rule. The
Queen-Mother was desirous of acting as Regent
during the minority of her son James the Third.
Buchanan puts into the mouth of Archbishop
Kennedy his views on this subject, which agreed
with those of Knox; and as this oration of Kennedy's is held to be the finest bit of writing in his
whole work, we shall give an extract from it. It
is too long to be quoted in full, but the exordium
will give an idea of its quality as a whole.

"Illustrious nobles, I earnestly desire that all
who intend to speak on the affairs of the Commonwealth, may be allowed to deliver their sentiments
freely and without offence; because, were observa-
tions meant for the public advantage, to be viewed
in the light of personalities, in our present circumstances, it would be difficult to utter a sentence,
amid such different aims and conflicting sentiments,

which would not incur the displeasure of some of
the parties. As for myself, in delivering my sentiments, I shall, as far as I can, give no one cause
to complain unless he be guilty. But while I
shall use the liberty I claim as my birthright,
moderately, so as not willingly to offend, at the
same time I shall not, through fear to displease or
a wish to flatter, pass any argument which can bear
upon the present question.

" I perceive there are two opinions which prevent
our concord. The one is held by those who think
that what belongs to the advantage of all, ought
to be left to the choice of all, and as all are met
to give their suffrages respecting an office which
embraces the safety of the whole kingdom, it is
unjust to exclude any one from the hope of attain-
ing that station, who attempts it by fair and
honourable means. The other is supported by
those who think injustice would be done to the
Queen, an illustrious princess and most accomplished lady, unless she should be preferred before
every other, to watch over the safety of her son,
and exercise the administration of the kingdom.
The sentiments of the first, which I decidedly

prefer, I shall notice last. The opinion of the others I approve so far.

" They think it derogatory to the dignity of the Queen, that anyone should come in competition with her for this honour, lest her rank, which ought to be esteemed, as it is in fact, most sacred, might seem to be degraded by contending with inferiors, and if this were a dispute about honour alone, and not about the safety of the kingdom, I should willingly and entirely accede to their sentiments; but when we are to determine a question to-day, which involves the life and fortune of every private individual, and the general preservation of the whole nation, I think all private interests should yield to this grand consideration, and therefore I earnestly request those who thus think, so to remember the dignity of the Queen, that they do not meanwhile forget the laws, the venerable institutions, and the general welfare of the country. If they can show that the laws allow, and public expedience admits of the tutelage of the King, and the Regency of the kingdom being vested in the Queen, they shall have my support; but if what they claim be pernicious to the public, destructive to the laws, and disgraceful to the Queen, I hope her highness first, and all loyal subjects will pardon me, if—while I would protect and hold sacred the rank and dignity of the Queen, so far as the laws and customs of our ancestors permit — I do not conceal what I think, or rather I speak freely, what I cannot suppress without a crime."

Buchanan was only six years of age when James the Fourth died, but he repeatedly assures us that for many of the facts stated in his account of that monarch's reign he had the testimony of eye-witnesses. His narrative, accordingly, from this period onwards may be regarded as practically that of a contemporary. Its value for that reason can never be discounted; the worst that can be said of it is, that the writer looked at the events which he records and the motives which he discovers through prejudiced eyes. He certainly had his likes and dislikes, and took a strong position against a person or a party when he was convinced that they were wrong. His record is of additional value from the fact that he was on intimate terms with many of the prime movers in the stirring events which he narrates, and that his knowledge and experience enabled him to understand better than most the matters which he helped to settle and which he afterwards described.

Every allowance should be made for the bitterness with which he writes of Cardinal Beaton, for that ecclesiastical dignitary was Buchanan's arch-enemy, and to him more than anyone else were due the hardship and misery of the poet's earlier life. The Cardinal made his native land impossible for Buchanan, and his malice pursued him through England and France to Portugal. The personal equation ought, perhaps, to have no place in history, but the writer's estimate of Beaton does not stand alone, it is supported by documentary evidence and by historians whose judgment is unbiassed. The house of Hamilton was equally detested by Buchanan ; the reason is found by some in the long-standing feud which existed between the Earl of Lennox, Buchanan's own chief, and the Hamiltons. Allowance must of course be made for the old clan feeling and the feudal relation which in those days unconsciously coloured a man's view of movements and events. But making every concession on this point, the

Hamiltons played a somewhat ignoble part during this period of Scottish history. They had always an eye on the throne, and the shifting policy which they pursued was dictated by personal ambition and interest. The events which followed the arrival of Queen Mary from France, especially the Revolution after the murder of Darnley, are recorded by Buchanan from the standpoint which he had already adopted in his *Detectio* and *De Jure*, and call for no further comment. His sense of fairness, even with regard to the chief actors in these great affairs, is admitted by his opponents. His estimate of the character of Mary of Guise is just and even sympathetic, and all that could possibly be said in defence of the Queen of Scots own conduct is narrated by him in the message which he credits Mary with having despatched to the Court of France.

Judged by modern standards, Buchanan's "History" may appear in many respects defective, but he is not to be blamed for failing to be in advance of his own times. His conception of History was that of the Humanists, who took the masterpieces of the ancient world as their models. Viewed in relation to them, the work of the great Scotsman was worthy of the unstinted applause with which it was at first received. The scientific or philosophic conception of History, with which we are familiar, was unknown to the ancients. They believed that all that was required of them was a clear narrative of events. They were for the most part unconscious of the demand which is made upon the Historian to probe causes, to discover motives, to unravel the tangled web of national life, and to show how there is a progress and a development which again find their explanation in a higher unity. It may be true that about the very time when Buchanan was writing his " History," a school of thinkers, with Bodin as its leader, was springing up in France which was to originate this deeper and modern conception of History. Buchanan was no doubt too old to adopt it; his mental training and habits were against it. He was a poet and a man of letters, who in later life was drawn into the vortex of political contention. His work, accordingly, must be judged in the light of his ideals, his character, and his preparation for his task. If he failed to see the full significance of

what he recorded, or was blind to the full bearings
of the great movements of his own day, if, to judge
from the few and brief references that are made to
Knox, he did not foresee the ampler estimate that
future generations would pass upon him, the explanation is to be found in those conditions
which limited the writer's insight and outlook
more than in any real defects in Buchanan
himself.

Much has been said in various quarters of the
inaccuracies of Buchanan's " History." Recent investigation has shown that they are not so numerous
as was at one time supposed. True, he was not a
critical, any more than he was a scientific or
philosophic historian; possibly he did not test the
value of documents as we are accustomed to do,
but it would be a mistake to forget that he had
access to sources of information which are not now
available. He had too strong convictions and too
deep feelings to treat History in a purely objective
manner, but he was too honest a man to wilfully
misrepresent facts, and too sane a thinker to
believe that truth could be vindicated or the
course of events diverted by a mis-statement of

them. Indeed, one of the chief aims of his History, as we have seen, was to controvert "English lies" and to prick the bladder of "Scottish vanity"; that he did not entirely succeed is simply to say that he was human. His work, however, made it easier for his successors to carry out his intention more fully; so that even from this point of view it was not in vain.

He is also accused of prejudice. This is true, if to be prejudiced is to be the champion of what one believes to be right, and the condemner of what one holds to be wrong. A man's moral sense may of course be blunted or perverted by partisanship, passion, or personal pique. Very few are entirely free of some subjective quality which more or less impairs their power of seeing the truth as it really is. Buchanan was no exception. He felt perhaps more keenly than most, and did not hesitate to express his convictions. His judgment of Queen Mary is held up as his great offence in this matter, but his view of the rights of the Crown and his belief in Mary's guilt inevitably led him to the conclusions which he had formed. If he expressed his opinions too strongly, let that be regarded as a failure in manners and not in morals.

Buchanan in a letter to Randolph says: "As for the present, I am occupied in writing of our history, being assured to content few and to displease many thereby." This forecast of the reception which was likely to be accorded to his work was only partially verified. It was cordially welcomed on its appearance, and passed rapidly through several editions. Many of the best spirits of the time welcomed it on its own account and for the sake of its author. Hallam, at a later date, praises its purity of language. "It is written," he says, "with strength, perspicuity, and neatness." "Few modern histories," he further remarks, "are more redolent of an antique air." The writer's anticipation of the unfavourable reception it would obtain on the part of a certain section of the public was not, however, altogether unwarranted. The political views which it advocated were very distasteful to those who believed in the divine right of kings, and James himself was indignant at the theories which it promulgated, and at its frank criticism of the conduct of his own mother. One result of this opposition was, as we have seen, its condemnation by Parliament in 1584; but it survived the storm and leavened the thought of the nation. It undoubtedly played its part in enlightening the public mind on those constitutional questions which are at the root of all civil government. Its importance in this respect cannot be overrated. This, along with the writer's narrative of the events of his own time, which was that of a contemporary, and in not a few instances of a witness, will always, apart from the intrinsic merits of the work itself, cause Buchanan's "History" to be taken account of by every author who attempts to tell the story of the Scottish nation.

CHAPTER XVI

THE biographer of Buchanan is under the disadvantage of not possessing those materials of a personal and intimate nature which throw more light on the character of a man than any formal document, however reliable. Familiar memoirs and letters in which special reference is made to him on the part of contemporaries are not very numerous, and he himself was characterised by a native reserve which interfered with that free communication of thought and emotion that reveal the true inwardness of a man. Samuel Johnson would never have been the figure that he is in English literature had it not been for Boswell, who minutely recorded the conversations of the dictator, and drew a portrait of him not only as the great writer, but as the man of moods, and whims, and fancies. The age of

Memoirs had just begun. Had Buchanan lived even half a century later, fuller knowledge of a personal nature regarding him would no doubt be in our hands; but fortunately in the two gossiping Memorials of the times that we possess, those of Sir James Melville of Halhill and of James Melville, Andrew's nephew, traits of character are recorded which bring Buchanan before us as a living reality, and not as a mere shadowy simulacrum. Sir James's sketch has already been given; it is to be accepted with reservation. The other, Melville's interview with Buchanan, will find a place in our concluding chapter.

From these and other testimonies, we find in Buchanan that simplicity and honesty of character which lie at the root of all true friendship. If our study of his life and work has been sound and just, we must see in him those qualities which, if they did not on the first blush attract men and win their confidence, would in the end attach to him kindred and worthy natures whose trust he would never betray. Indeed, this is what we do find.

His life must have been lonely in many respects, but very few men of his own day had so many and so distinguished friends. Nor do we hear of any of them falling away or turning against him, with the exception of those whom he necessarily estranged by the side which he took in the popular crusade against Queen Mary, and even they must have been few in number. The friends of his youth and manhood remained constant to the very end, and addressed him in terms of respect and admiration such as are accorded only to those who have proved worthy. We have seen how Knox spoke of him, and his regard, in turn, for the great Reformer was equally sincere. Andrew Melville revered him as his master, and the Earl of Moray treated him as a personal friend. We have also seen how at the very beginning of his career he drew to him some of the finest spirits and greatest scholars in the University of Paris; and as his fame spread the number of admirers increased, and their admiration soon passed into a close and loyal friendship. A glance at his poems is sufficient to show the warm response he made to their devotion. He paid back in golden coin their loyal homage.

The chief editor of Buchanan's works publishes forty-one letters that passed between him and his

17

friends. Only fourteen of these are by Buchanan. The correspondence shows the wide circle of his friendship and the high position in the world of letters which his friends occupied. Their names have already occurred in the course of this narrative, and it may be unnecessary to repeat them again, but when we find among them such men as Beza, Gouvéa, Turnèbe, Tycho Brahé, Scaliger, Sturm, Randolph, Ascham, Languet, and others, the list of European celebrities of the time in the field of scholarship is pretty well exhausted. All of them write to Buchanan in terms of affection and reverence, and he replies with a simplicity and directness which show his letters to be no studied or formal productions, but the intimate correspondence of a friend. Indeed, as Dr. Hume Brown points out, that is a very marked feature of Buchanan's letters. They were not written for effect, as was the habit then and for a good time afterwards; they were the respectful and kindly communications of one who had something to say, and said it in the simplest and most direct manner possible. He was not a correspondent of the type of Erasmus. He did not go raging or wailing over

Europe taking the whole world into his confidence. His Scottish reserve would not allow him to carry his heart on his sleeve. This, of course, prevents his letters from being so informative or interesting as those of Erasmus. The world is so much the poorer on that account, but it is doubtful if Buchanan's character or reputation has suffered thereby. We would not, all the same, wish Buchanan or Erasmus to be other than he was.

One of the most pleasing features in these letters is the deep interest which Buchanan had in the young Scottish scholars who were pursuing their studies on the Continent. He writes to his friends who were on the teaching staff of the Institutions where these lads were studying, soliciting their interest on their behalf, and when he himself is asked to render similar service to any foreigner visiting Scotland, the request was evidently not made in vain.

It may serve our purpose best to give, instead of going through the correspondence as a whole, two letters from the collection, one addressed to him by Hubert Languet, and another by Buchanan himself to his old friend and former colleague, Elias

Vinet. They will afford an indication of the relation that existed between Buchanan and his friends, and the manner in which they addressed each other.

Languet was a man after Buchanan's own heart, at once Humanist and Reformer, with a sagacity and judgment which gave him considerable influence with the Elector of Saxony and the Prince of Orange. He was a Frenchman, but his religious opinions compelled him to seek refuge in Germany. He travelled much, and latterly made Holland his home. He died at Antwerp in September 1581. The letter is somewhat long, but well worth quoting almost in full.

" By your virtue, and by the various and noble monuments of your genius, you have rendered yourself so conspicuous in the Christian world, that hardly a single lover of science and literature can be found who does not regard you with the utmost reverence and admiration. I consider it as an instance of no common felicity, that about twenty years ago it was my lot not only to see you at Paris, and to enjoy your most pleasant and most learned conversation, but also to entertain you as my guest, together with those distinguished men,

Turnèbe, Dorat, and some others. We then heard you discuss various subjects in a manner which tended very much to our edification and delight. To these circumstances I now allude, for the purpose of trying whether I can suggest to your recollection who I am : but whoever I am, assure yourself of my being a warm admirer of your virtue. For several years I lived with Philip Melanchthon, and I then seemed to myself to live happily.

" Having after his decease been exposed to various chances, I have at length betaken myself to these regions, as to a haven more secure than any other that I could find, notwithstanding their having been agitated for many years by the storms of civil war. Even amidst these warlike tumults, the light of the gospel shines forth ; to us is announced the doctrine which points out the true path of salvation ; and while the Spaniards threaten destruction, the super-stition which infects their minds is expelled from the churches. It was the Prince of Orange, the great ornament of our age, who commanded me to accompany him to this place. Supported by the vigour and acuteness of his mind, he has hitherto maintained such a contest with the formidable power

of the Spaniards, as has procured him immortal
glory. After having under his auspices severed
their tyrannical empire, these provinces have happily
constituted various republics and churches, which,
being closely leagued together, have hitherto resisted
the attacks of the enemy. The King of Spain
having for several years endeavoured without success
to overwhelm him by force, has at length resorted
to weapons which do not seem altogether worthy of
so great a monarch; he has issued an edict in which
he pronounces sentence of prescription, and en-
deavours, by proposing rewards, to impel assassins
to accomplish his murder. Since many falsehoods
are there alleged against him, he has been advised
by his friends to publish an apology, for the purpose
of vindicating his innocence against the calumnies
of the Spaniards. This apology I transmit to
you.

" During the winter, I have lived in these puddles
of the Dutch, which nature seems rather to have
intended for the habitation of frogs and eels than
of men. This town is, however, very handsome ;
and at the distance of three hours' journey stands
Leyden, or *Lugdunum Batavorum*, as they now

speak, the residence of Justus Lipsius, Janus Dousa the poet, and Donellus the French jurisconsult, men of learning and celebrity. From the vicinity of this town we have a prospect of Rotterdam; a prospect which not only recalls to my memory the great Erasmus, in whom it glories as a citizen, but also you: for I cannot sufficiently express my astonishment, that such horrid places should produce men to whose talents neither our own age, nor that of our fathers or grandfathers, has exhibited a parallel. Erasmus was invited to instruct the youth of Ferdinand, brother to the Emperor Charles, but he declined this employment. I account you more fortunate and virtuous in not having refused to aid your country, when it called you to imbue the King's tender mind with those precepts which, being observed in his riper years, will secure the happiness and prosperity of himself, and of all those to whom his dominion extends. I am very anxious to learn, provided it should not be disagreeable to you, when you shall publish your "Scottish History." From Melville, an excellent man, you may know the state of my affairs. Farewell."

Vinet, to whom Buchanan addresses the following

letter, was his colleague at the Collége de Guyenne, Bordeaux, and subsequently at Coimbra in Portugal. They had been friends in youth, and after nearly half a century of toil and trouble they were friends still. It was the last letter but one of which we have any record that Buchanan wrote, and de Thou, to whom Vinet showed it, says "it was written in a trembling hand but magnanimous spirit."

"Upon receiving accounts of you by the merchants who returned from your coasts, I am filled with delight, and seem to enjoy a kind of second youth; for I am apprised that a remnant still survives of our notable Portuguese expedition. As I have now attained to the seventy-fifth year of my age, I sometimes call to remembrance through what cares and toils I have sailed past all those ports which men commonly regard as pleasing, and have at length struck upon that rock beyond which (as the ninetieth Psalm very truly avers) nothing remains but labour and sorrow. The only consolation which now awaits me, is to pause with delight on the recollection of my friends, of whom you are almost the only one who still survives. Although

you are not, as I presume, younger than me in
years, you are yet capable of benefiting your country
by your exertion and counsel, and even of prolonging,
by your learned compositions, your life to a future
age. But I have long bade adieu to letters. It is
now the only object of my solicitude that I may
remove, with as little noise as possible, from a
generation with which I am no longer in sympathy;
that I, as one dead, may leave the haunts of the
living.

" In the meantime, I transmit to you the youngest
of my literary offspring, in order that when you
discover it to be the drivelling child of age, you
may be less anxious about its brothers. I understand that Henry Wardlaw, a young man of our
nation, and the descendant of a good family, is
prosecuting his studies in your seminary with no
inconsiderable application. Although I am aware
of your habitual politeness, and you are not ignorant
that foreigners are peculiarly entitled to your attention, yet I am desirous he should find that our
ancient friendship recommends him to your favour."

The one man, so far as any evidence remains, with
whom Buchanan during the latter part of his life

was on the most friendly footing, was Sir Thomas
Randolph, the English resident at the Scottish
Court. They knew each other on the Continent,
and their friendship was renewed after Buchanan's
return to his native land. It was largely owing to
pressure on the part of Randolph that Buchanan
wrote the Latin Sketch of his Life, and in the few
letters that remain of their correspondence we get
some glimpses, brief but luminous, of Buchanan
when, in friendly undress, so to speak, he indulged
in those witty and humorous sallies for which he
was noted. No better specimen of this vein in his
genius has been preserved than a letter from him
to Randolph, first printed by Dr. M'Crie in the
Appendix to his *Life of Andrew Melville.*

The English resident who had risked matrimony
for the second time, had evidently been urging his
old friend to renounce bachelorhood, and, particularly in view of his growing infirmities, to take
a wife. To this, and to other matters, Buchanan
replies in the following letter, which in addition to
its value as a bit of self-revelation, shows us how he
could write in the original Scots :

To his singular Freynd M. Randolph Maister of Postes to the queines g. of Ingland. In london.

"I resauit twa pair of lettres of you sens my latter wryting to you. wyth the fyrst I ressauit Marianus Scotus, of quhylk I thank you greatly, and specialy that your ingles men are fund liars in their cronicles allegying on hym sic thyngs as he never said. I haif beyne vexit wyth seikness al the tyme sens, and geif I had decessit ye suld haif losit both thankis and recompens, now I most neid thank you bot geif wear brekks vp of thys foly laitly done on the border, than I wyl hald the recompense as Inglis geir. bot gif peace followis and nother ye die seik of mariage or of the twa symptomes following on mariage quhylks ar jalozie [and] cuccaldry, and the gut carry not me away, I most other find sum way to pay or ceis kyndnes or ellis geifing vp kyndness pay zou w^t evil wordis, and geif thys fasson of dealing pleasit me I haif reddy occasion to be angry wyth you that haif wissit me to be ane kentys man, quylk in a manner in ane centaur, half man half beast. and yit for ane certaine consideration I

wyl pas over that iniury, imputyng it erar to your
new foly than to ald wisdome, for geif ye had beine
in your ryt wyt ye being anis escapit the tempestuous
stormes and naufrage of mariage had never enterit
agane in the samyng dangeris. for I can not take
you for ane Stoik philosopher having ane head
inexpugnable w^t the frenetyk tormētis of Jalozie,
or ane cairless [*margin*, skeptik] hart that taks
cuccaldris as thyng indifferent. In this caise I most
neidis præfer the rude Scottis wyt of capitaine
cockburne to your inglis solomonical sapience,
quhylk wery of ane wyfe deliuerit hir to the queyne
againe, bot you deliuerit of ane wyfe castis your self
in the samyn nette, *et ferre potes dominam saluis
tot restibus ullam.* and so capitaine cockburne is in
better case than you for his seiknes is in the feitte
and youris in the heid. I pray you geif I be out of
purpose thynk not that I suld be maryit. bot
rather consider your awyn dangerous estait of the
quhylk the spoking has thus troublit my braine and
put me so far out of the way. As to my occupation at
the present tyme, I am besy w^t our story of Scotland
to purge it of sum Inglis lyis and Scottis vanite; as
to maister knoks his historie is in hys friendis hands,

and thai ar in cōsultation to mitigat sum part the
acerbite of certaine wordis and sum taintis quhair in
he has followit to much sū of your inglis writairs as
M. hal *et suppilatorem eius* Graftone, &c.   As to M.
beza I fear yᵗ eild quhylk has put me from verses
making sal deliure him sone a Scabie poetica,
quhylk war ane great pitye for he is ane of the most
singular poetes that has beine thys lang tyme.   as
to your great prasyng gevin to me in your lře geif
ye scorne not I thank you of luif and kyndnes
towart me, bot I am sorie of your corrupt iugement.
heir I wald say mony iniuries to you war not yat
my gut cōmandis me to cesse and I wyl als spair
mater to my nixt writings. Fairweall and god
keip you.   At Sterling the Sext of august.

"Be youris at al power,

"G. Buchanan."

CHAPTER XVII

THE END

IN the letter—quoted in the last Chapter—which Buchanan wrote to his friend and former colleague Vinet, he speaks of himself as an old man whose interest in life was rapidly passing away. He was then in his seventy-fifth year, having, as he forcibly puts it, "in my voyage of life at length struck on that rock beyond which, as it is most truly said in the ninetieth Psalm, nothing remains but labour and sorrow." Indeed, he had only one year more to live; and this letter was most probably written in the last house occupied by him, and the one in which he died. This was in Kennedy's Close, the second close off the High Street of Edinburgh above the Tron Church. His lodging, according to George Paton the antiquary, was in the first court in the close on the left hand, "first house in the turnpike above the tavern there." This lodging, remarks Sheriff Campbell Smith, "occupied some few cubic feet of space, probably about twelve feet above the existing causeway blocks of Hunter Square, an entirely vanished pile of tall, substantial, over-populated masonry, part of the crest of the High Street, once standing within a quarter of a mile of the vanished garden in which Darnley was found dead in his shirt without mark of violence, still nearer to the site of the vanished house in which Walter Scott was born, and to the vacant air space once filled by Johnny Dowie's vanished tavern, in which during his Edinburgh sojourn Robert Burns was wont to make merry with select friends." Here Buchanan busied himself with seeing his " History " through the press, and here he received a visit in September of 1581, a year before his death, from Andrew and James Melville and Buchanan's own cousin, Thomas Buchanan, who "crossed from St. Andrews to Edinburgh with the express purpose of visiting the old scholar." James Melville has given in his Diary an account of the interview, which in the opinion of Dr. Hume Brown "is not only a vivid page of biography, but has in it a strain that reminds us of Plutarch at his best."

"That September in tyme of vacans, my uncle Mr. Andro, Mr. Thomas Buchanan, and I, heiring that Mr. George Buchanan was weak and his Historie under the pres, past ower to Edinburche annes errand, to visit him and sie the wark. When we cam to his chalmer we fand him sitting in his chaire, teatching his young man that servit him in his chalmer to spell a, b, ab; e, b, eb, etc. Efter salutation, Mr. Andro sayes, 'I sie, sir, yie are nocht ydle.'

"'Better this,' quoth he, 'nor stelling sheipe, or sitting ydle, quhilk is als ill.'

"Therefter he schew us the Epistle Dedicatorie to the King, the quhilk, when Mr. Andro had read, he tauld him that it was obscure in sum places, and wanted certean words to perfyt the sentence.

"Says he, 'I may do na mair for thinking on another mater.'

"'What is that?' says Mr. Andro.

"'To die!' quoth he; 'bot I leave that and manie ma things for you to helpe.'

"We went from him to the printar's work house,

whom we fand at the end of the 17 buik of his Cronicle at a place quhilk we thought verie hard for the tyme, quhilk might be an occasion of steying the haill wark, anent the buriall of Davie [Rizzio]. Therfor, steying the printer from proceiding, we cam to Mr. George again, and fund him bedfast by [contrary to] his custome, and asking him whow he did, 'Even going the way of weilfare,' says he. Mr. Thomas, his cusing, schawes him of the hardness of that part of his Storie, that the King wald be offendit with it, and it might stey all the wark.

"'Tell me, man,' sayes he, 'giff I have tauld the treuthe?'

"'Yis,' sayes Mr. Thomas; 'sir, I think sa.'

"'I will byd his fead and all his Kins, then,' quoth he: 'Pray, pray to God for me, and let him direct all.'

"Sa, be the printing of his Cronicle was endit, that maist lerned, wyse, and godlie man, endit this his mortall lyff."

A little later, when the end was drawing near, another interview took place, this time between Buchanan and his own servant, which is quite as characteristic of the old scholar as the one just

18

recorded, and which bears out Sir James Melville's description of him as "a Stoick philosopher, who looked not far before him."

"When Buchanan was dying," so runs the story as told by Mackenzie in his *Lives of Scots Worthies*, "he called Mr. Young, his servant, and asked him how much money he had of his; and finding that it was not sufficient for defraying the charges of his burial, he commanded him to distribute it among the poor. Upon which Mr. Young, asking who then would be at the charges of burying him, he answered that he was very indifferent about that, for if he was once dead, if they would not bury him, they might let him lie where he was, or throw his corpse where they pleased; and that accordingly the city of Edinburgh was obliged to bury him at their own expenses."

Other stories have gathered round Buchanan's deathbed, two of them credibly vouched for, and they are so characteristic of the man that little doubt has been entertained of their truth. That persecution of his memory which in after years exhibited itself in the condemnation of his opinions and the burning of his books, almost overtook him before he died. The authorities had even gone the length of summoning him to answer for something objectionable in his writings, but he was unmoved. "Tell the people who sent you," was his reply to the macer of the Court of Session who came on the errand, "that I am summoned to a higher Tribunal." A Presbyterian minister, one John Davidson, visited him for the purpose of strengthening his faith, should it be drooping, and confirming him in the doctrines of the Reformed religion. He gave the necessary assurance, and gratified the good Presbyter's soul with a humorous sally at the expense of the Romish doctrine of the Mass.

The end came on the 28th of September 1582. The Town Council of Edinburgh manifested no unseemly delay in burying their distinguished citizen. The funeral took place on the following day, which was a Saturday, and it was "attended by a great company of the faithful." Buchanan judged right in predicting a public funeral, so far at least as the expenses were concerned. He left nothing but his pension, and that, as was not unfrequent, had not been paid. He was buried in the grounds of Greyfriars, which had recently been opened up as a

cemetery, and he was the first " person of celebrity "
to find a resting-place there. A stone without an
inscription would seem to have been the only monument that was erected to mark his grave. After a
time it disappeared, and on being discovered was
made use of as a tombstone for a gravedigger. A
humble blacksmith erected a tablet, at his own
expense, where Buchanan is supposed to be buried.
More recently a monument, in the shape of a large
pedestal, with a life-sized bust, was erected in another
part of the churchyard. This, with a memorial
window in old Greyfriars Church, an obelisk in
Killearn, and a bust in the Wallace Monument at
Stirling, is all that Scotland has done to show its
appreciation of its greatest scholar, and one of its
most outstanding personalities.

Many portraits exist of Buchanan, and several
descriptions of his appearance have been handed
down to us. He had the head of a scholar, dome-
shaped ; and his features, especially the mouth and
chin, betoken strength and character. He is said to
have been " austere in face and rustic in his looks, but
most polished in style and speech, and continually,
even in serious conversation, jesting most wittily."

"Rough hewn," says Peacham in his *Compleat Gentleman*, speaking of him as he appeared in his old age, "in his person, behaviour, and fashion, seldom caring for a better outside than a rugge-gown girt close about him; yet his inside and conceit in poesy was most rich, and his sweetness and facilities in verse most excellent." "He was," says Sir James Melville, "pleasant in conversation, rehearsing at all occasion moralities, short and instructive, whereof he had abundance, inventing where he wanted." According to Daniel Heinsius, "he was one who seemed not only born for a court, but born to amend it. He brought to his Queen that at which she could not wonder enough. For by affecting a certain liberty in censuring morals, he avoided all offence under the cloak of simplicity."

These passages give us not only a description of Buchanan's appearance, but some idea of the esteem in which he was held by his contemporaries. Reference has already been made to the high opinion that was formed of his abilities and character by some of the leading scholars of his day, and that opinion was reiterated by not a few of their distin-

guished successors, such as Roger Ascham and Sir
Philip Sidney in the sixteenth century, and by Milton
and Cowley in the seventeenth.   Dryden, at a later
date, declared that as a " historian he was comparable to any of the moderns, and excelled by few of the
ancients."   Warton characterised him as " a popular
modern classic."   " What would you have said,"
inquired a certain Scotsman once of Dr. Johnson,
" had Buchanan been an Englishman ? "   " Why, Sir,"
replied the great dictator, " I should not have said,
had he been an Englishman, what I will say of him
as a Scotchman, that he was the only man of genius
whom his country ever produced."   Johnson's opinion
was probably not far wrong, if we take into account
the time at which it was given.   Hume, Adam
Smith, Burns, Scott, and Carlyle had not as yet taken
their place among the *Dii majores* of literature, and
Buchanan was certainly at the time the chief representative of the Scottish nation in the world of
letters.   " The Scottish genius," remarks Mr. James
Hannay, " had *brairded* before his day, but had never
ripened into grain to be eaten as bread.   It was he
who made us famous, from the Vistula to the Tagus,
and gave us a national name in literature by his pen,

as Bruce had given us a national name in the politics by his sword."

It was certainly by his genius that Buchanan accomplished all this. The popular idea of him as a great Latin scholar, who could equal the Romans themselves in his mastery over their tongue, could never of itself have gained for him the position which he held, and still holds, in the world of letters. Nor was he a mere philologist, like Scaliger or Casaubon, who expended all their force in the critical elucidation of classical authors. He was a thinker as well as a scholar, and his wealth of ideas and power of observation saved him from being a mere pedant. He made use of the Latin language as a means for expressing in literary form his reflections on men and things. We agree with Dr. Hume Brown's estimate of him as a man of letters, who was more concerned in criticising, expounding, and influencing the thought of his time than in presenting to his contemporaries a corrected and pure text of the writers of classical antiquity. His knowledge of the ancient writers and of the language in which they wrote was, to say the least, equal to that of the first scholars of his time, but he found a higher use for that knowledge. Just as the greatest poets, who are masters of the language in which they write, make use of it for the purpose of conveying their highest thought, and not as the ground for writing dictionaries or works on syntax or prosody, so Buchanan was content to leave the useful though humbler task of the enlightened grammarian to others, preferring to devote himself to the higher work of interpreting to the age in which he lived its own ideals and destiny.

Buchanan, besides, differentiated himself from the majority of his literary contemporaries by being a man of affairs. He took a practical interest in the movements of the times, and played his part in carrying to a successful issue the questions in which he was interested. This is particularly true of the last part of his career. He associated himself with Knox and his fellow-Reformers in putting the affairs of the Church on a business footing, and with Moray and the other progressive politicians in carrying through the Revolution which followed on the deposition of Mary. His interest in education was wholehearted and continuous. Indeed, it may be said that the training of youth was the serious business of his life. He began his active career as Regent in Ste. Barbe, and he ended it as tutor to King James. The fact of him being thus a man of the world, in the best sense of the word, gave a reality to his writings which they might not otherwise have possessed. It may be true that many of the subjects on which he wrote were artificial and ephemeral; they were topics of the hour, or chosen at the promptings of that Humanism which, to a large extent, found its themes in the past. But in Buchanan's handling of them there is a touch of common sense which gives them an air of reality even still. It is, however, when he deals with questions which were of vital and practical concern, or which were true to the intellect and imagination, that we find him at his best, and on the rare occasions on which his genius spreads its wings we find it soaring to heights that can only be reached by the greatest.

It may be difficult to say in what particular form of writing he chiefly excelled. As a matter of fact he shone in everything he attempted. This is saying a great deal, for in poetry alone he wrote on every kind of theme, and attempted every variety of metre. In the opinion of some he excelled as a satirist; but his satire was not of that light vein which we associate with Aristophanes and Horace, but of the strong and serious sort represented by such writers as Juvenal and Swift. His masculine intellect, sardonic humour, and intense earnestness lent themselves to a production like *Franciscanus*, his chief example in this form of writing. But, as we have seen, he could, on occasion, be as playful and light and witty as Horace, and he was able, as in his Ode on the "First of May," to give rein to imaginative powers that give him a title to take a place in the higher ranks of poetry. As a writer of prose he aimed at clearness and force, seldom indulged in rhetorical flourishes, and if in his " History " there be purple patches they are spontaneous and not manufactured.

Buchanan found himself at the meeting of the waters of the old world and the new. It must stand to his lasting credit that in the collision which took place between tradition and enlightenment he invariably took the side which made for liberty. He was from the very first an advocate of that Humanism which was to free the mind of his age from the thraldom of the Scholastic philosophy and learning, and to start it on a course of ever-increasing progress. He advocated the rights of the nation in opposition to that absolutism which was one of the signs of the times; but while putting a limit to the rights of the Crown he was no friend of mob rule, and no believer in giving to the ignorant majority unlimited power. He would apply to government by the people those constitutional restrictions in the observance of which the rights of the whole nation can alone be conserved and defended. He had also made his choice between the Roman and Protestant views of the Christian religion and Church. His sympathies were from the very first undoubtedly on the side of the Reformers, but it was only after careful study and consideration that he came into the open and publicly identified himself with the movement which they championed. But he was no fanatic; his religion was that of a thoughtful and cultured man who believed that absolute truth was not to be found in any Church or creed, and that the reverent soul might be unable to put in dogmatic form the sum and substance of its faith. All the same, he found in the Protestant religion a truer interpretation of the mind and spirit of Christ than in Roman Catholicism, which had in his day degenerated into what appeared to every serious-minded man, an almost hopeless condition. Salvation for the individual and the nation could never, at anyrate, be found in it. Man's spiritual needs demanded the new form of the Christian Faith represented by Protestantism.

The influence of Buchanan upon his own age can hardly be exaggerated. He was a European celebrity, and his name was one to conjure with for many years after he died. If he has suffered eclipse, it is chiefly, we think, because of the language in which he wrote and the themes which circumstances suggested to him. As a political force, however, he still lives far beyond the shores of his native country. The spirit of liberty which breathes through his *De Jure* and his "History" can never die, but will, so long as man exists, find expression in the assertion of those rights which inherently belong to him. With regard, however, to his own country, it is different. Buchanan is still, and will, we believe, always continue to be, one of Scotland's dominant personalities. He was for many generations the inspirer of Scottish youth, and presented to them an ideal in the world of literature and learning which it was their aim to realise. With Buchanan as their compatriot they as Scotsmen could hold up their heads in face of the most learned nations of the world. His genius, his accomplishments, his works were their glory and their pride. But greater than all these is the character of Buchanan, which in its simplicity, honesty, and noble ideals is a possession of incomparable worth. He despised wealth, he never courted fame; all he desired was liberty to do his work. That work was of the highest order; and the fact that he accomplished it in spite of hardship, persecution, and poverty, before which the most indomitable courage might have broken down, inspires us with a deep sense of the greatness of the man and the iron resolution which enabled him to prevail, and in the end to conquer. In these times of uncertain aims and imperfect fulfilment, the spirit of George Buchanan calls Scottish youth to the realisation of a truer manhood and a nobler life.

INDEX

Printed by MORRISON & GIBB LIMITED, *Edinburgh*

SELECT LIST

OF

PUBLICATIONS

NEW IDEAS IN INDIA

DURING THE NINETEENTH CENTURY.

A STUDY OF SOCIAL, POLITICAL, AND RELIGIOUS DEVELOPMENTS.

BY

REV. JOHN MORRISON, M.A., D.D.,

Late Principal, The General Assembly's Institution, Church of Scotland
Mission, Calcutta, and Member of Senate of Calcutta University.

Large Crown 8vo, with a Map.

It is the popular belief that there are no new ideas in India;
that nought in India suffers change; that as things are so they
have always been. The author of "New Ideas in India" com-
pares the position now with what it was a century ago, and shows
that to the observant student of the Indian people the evolution of
India is almost as noteworthy as the more apparent rigidity.

The seeds of the "New Ideas in India" during the past century
are the outcome of British influence, direct or indirect, and one of
the results of the writer's study of the subject is that there is a call
for some one to interpret Britain and India to each other. Britain's
views are often incomplete and distorted. And on the Indian side
the anti-British feeling is based on ignorance and misunderstanding,
and in part, at least, removable.

EDINBURGH: GEO. A. MORTON, 42 GEORGE STREET.
LONDON: SIMPKIN, MARSHALL, & CO. LTD.

2

FUTURE LIFE

IN THE LIGHT OF MODERN SCIENCE
AND ANCIENT WISDOM.

BY

LOUIS ELBÉ.

AUTHORISED ENGLISH TRANSLATION.

Large crown 8vo.

———————

This is the Authorised English Translation of Louis Elbé's
"La Vie Future"—a work which, when published in Paris
recently, created a tremendous stir in scientific and religious
circles throughout France.

The fundamental question of "The Immortality of the Soul"
has disturbed the great thinkers of all ages, and for the solution
of this eternal enigma humanity still seeks in vain; and in "The
Future Life," M. Elbé presents a mass of scientific evidence that
is startling and convincing.

The book is divided into two parts, the first being devoted to
the Idea of the Survival, as considered by the Primitive Races,
and the second to Deductions drawn from the Fundamental
Sciences.

———————

EDINBURGH : GEO. A. MORTON, 42 GEORGE STREET.
LONDON : SIMPKIN, MARSHALL, & CO. LTD.

SECOND EDITION, REVISED AND ENLARGED.

RAMBLES WITH A FISHING ROD.

BY

E. S. ROSCOE.

With Eight Illustrations.

Large crown 8vo, pp. 256, price 5s.

The sketches are the result of some vacations chiefly spent in rambling about the Continent with a fishing-rod. These expeditions were not undertaken with the businesslike and earnest energy with which we go a-fishing in this country, if we make it the chief object of a holiday, be it of a day or a month. The book is not intended to guide the reader over this or that district —rather to incite him to find his way for himself.

EDINBURGH : GEO. A. MORTON, 42 GEORGE STREET.
LONDON : SIMPKIN, MARSHALL, & CO. LTD.

4

MY SCHOOLS AND SCHOOLMASTERS;

Or, THE STORY OF MY EDUCATION.

By HUGH MILLER,

Author of "The Old Red Sandstone,"
"Footprints of the Creator," etc.

With an Introduction and Notes by

W. M. MACKENZIE, M.A., F.S.A. (Scot.).

With Eight Page Illustrations.

Large crown 8vo, pp. 576, price 3s. 6d.

OF THIS WORK CARLYLE WROTE:—

"*Luminous, memorable: all wholesome, strong, fresh, and breezy, like the 'Old Red Sandstone Mountains' on a sunny summer day; it is really a long while since I have read a Book worthy of so much recognition from me, or likely to be so interesting to sound-hearted men of every degree.*"

UNIFORM WITH THE ABOVE.

SELECTIONS FROM THE WORKS OF HUGH MILLER. Arranged, with Notes, by W. M. MACKENZIE. With Illustrations. Large crown 8vo, price 3s. 6d.

EDINBURGH: GEO. A. MORTON, 42 GEORGE STREET.
LONDON: SIMPKIN, MARSHALL, & CO. LTD.

6

SECOND EDITION (FOURTH IMPRESSION),
REVISED AND ENLARGED.

THE KEEPER'S BOOK.

A GUIDE TO THE DUTIES OF A GAMEKEEPER.

BY

A. STODART WALKER

AND

P. JEFFREY MACKIE.

With Special Chapters by Lord DOUGLAS GRAHAM, Captain SHAW KENNEDY, Dr. CHARLES REID, JOHN LAMB, P. D. MALLOCH, HENRY LAMOND, TOM SPEEDY, and others.

With a Frontispiece.

Crown 8vo, price 5s. net.

"We have seldom read a better, more succinct, or more practical treatise. . . . It is an acquisition to the keeper's bookshelf, which should be in every gun-room."—*Times.*

"We are glad to welcome 'The Keeper's Book.' . . . Much practical advice is given."—*Field.*

"A complete *vade mecum* for the British gamekeeper." — *County Gentleman.*

"Eminently practical."—*Pall Mall Gazette.*

EDINBURGH: GEO. A. MORTON, 42 GEORGE STREET.
LONDON: SIMPKIN, MARSHALL, & CO. LTD.

7

THE LIFE-HISTORY

OF

BRITISH LIZARDS

AND THEIR LOCAL DISTRIBUTION
IN THE BRITISH ISLES.

BY

GERALD R. LEIGHTON, M.D., F.R.S.E.,
Author of "British Serpents," etc.

With numerous Illustrations from Photographs of Living Lizards
by DOUGLAS ENGLISH, and from original Drawings.

Crown 8vo, price 5s. net.

"A wonderfully interesting book. . . . Indispensable to every field naturalist."—*Morning Leader.*

"The book is throughout accurate and painstaking. . . . The photographs which accompany the text are singularly happy."—*Morning Post.*

"Dr. Leighton has the advantage of a fascinating and a manageable subject. . . . It is perfectly clear, and is easily understandable, and yet it is thoroughly scientific. . . . To the field naturalist it will be invaluable."—*Manchester Courier.*

"Tells all about Lizards that a field naturalist on the look-out for them, or curious as to their ways of life, needs to know. Handy, concise, and clearly expounded. . . . Serviceable and instructive to all classes."—*Scotsman.*

EDINBURGH: GEO. A. MORTON, 42 GEORGE STREET.
LONDON: SIMPKIN, MARSHALL, & CO. LTD,

8

SCOTTISH PEWTER-WARE AND PEWTERERS.

By L. INGLEBY WOOD.

Crown 4to.

With 36 Collotype Plates and other Illustrations.

Tastefully Bound in Art Cloth, Gilt.

Price 15s. net.

"A mine of information which no collector of pewter can afford to be without."—*Studio.*

"Well written, well edited, crammed with facts, and profusely illustrated."—*The Collector's Illustrated.*

"Will be of much assistance to collectors. . . . The volume teems with interesting details relating to the pewterer's art."—*Daily Telegraph.*

"Mr. Ingleby Wood's book is interesting in many ways. The illustrations are among the best we have ever seen."—*Morning Post.*

"There has not appeared as yet any work on the subject comparable in point of erudition and beauty of form to Mr. Ingleby Wood's. . . . A splendid addition to the collector's library."—*Bookman.*

EDINBURGH : GEO. A. MORTON, 42 GEORGE STREET.
LONDON : SIMPKIN, MARSHALL, & CO. LTD.

CHURCH OF SCOTLAND.

THE GUILD LIBRARY AND THE GUILD TEXT-BOOKS.

Edited by Very Rev. A. H. CHARTERIS, D.D., LL.D.,
Emeritus Professor of Biblical Criticism, Edinburgh
University, and Rev. J. A. M'CLYMONT, D.D.,
Aberdeen.

THE GUILD LIBRARY.

In crown 8vo Volumes, cloth, gilt back, price 1s. 6d. net each.

* RELIGIONS OF THE WORLD.
By the late Principal GRANT, D.D., LL.D., Queen's
University, Canada. 34th Thousand.

* HANDBOOK OF CHRISTIAN EVIDENCES.
By Principal STEWART, D.D., University of St.
Andrews. 28th Thousand.

* THE NEW TESTAMENT AND ITS
WRITERS.
By Rev. J. A. M'CLYMONT, D.D., Aberdeen. 50th
Thousand.

* THE OLD TESTAMENT AND ITS
CONTENTS.
By Professor ROBERTSON, D.D., University of Glasgow. 34th Thousand.

* LANDMARKS OF CHURCH HISTORY.
By Professor COWAN, D.D., University of Aberdeen.
23rd Thousand.

* HISTORY OF THE CHURCH OF
SCOTLAND.
By Rev. P. M'ADAM MUIR, D.D., Glasgow. 27th
Thousand, including a Note on the decision in the
U.F. Church Case.

* OUR LORD'S TEACHING.
 By Rev. J. ROBERTSON, D.D., Whittinghame.
 37th Thousand.

* THE PRESBYTERIAN CHURCHES:
 Their Place and Power in Modern Christendom. By
 Rev. J. N. OGILVIE, M.A., New Greyfriars, Edinburgh.
 12th Thousand.

A FAITHFUL CHURCHMAN.
 Sketch of the Life and Work of Professor JAMES
 ROBERTSON, D.D. By Very Rev. A. H. CHARTERIS,
 D.D., LL.D.

THE PREPARATION FOR CHRISTIANITY
  IN THE ANCIENT WORLD.
 By R. M. WENLEY, Sc.D., D.Phil., Senior Pro-
 fessor of Philosophy in the University of Michigan.

THE MISSIONARY EXPANSION OF THE
  REFORMED CHURCHES.
 By the Rev. J. A. GRAHAM, M.A., D.D., Guild Mission-
 ary at Kalimpong. With 8 Maps and 145 Illustrations.

HYMNS AND HYMN MAKERS.
 By the late Rev. DUNCAN CAMPBELL, B.D., Edinburgh. Third Edition.

* BIBLE MANNERS AND CUSTOMS.
 By the Rev. GEORGE M. MACKIE, D.D., Beyrout.
 With Illustrations. 13th Thousand.

HANDBOOK OF CHRISTIAN ETHICS.
 By Prof. DAVIDSON, LL.D., University of Aberdeen. Second Edition.

SCOTTISH CATHEDRALS AND ABBEYS.
 By Rev. D. BUTLER, M.A., Tron Church, Edin-
 burgh. With Introduction by Very Rev. Principal
 STORY, D.D., LL.D.

ENGLISH RELIGIOUS WRITERS.
 By Rev. PEARSON M'ADAM MUIR, D.D., Glasgow.

THE GUILD TEXT-BOOKS.

Fcap. 8vo, paper covers, price 6d. net each.

All the Volumes of the GUILD LIBRARY marked * are to be had in the Sixpenny form with reduced contents.

LIFE AND CONDUCT.

By Very Rev. J. CAMERON LEES, D.D., LL.D., Dean of the Chapel Royal of Scotland. 35th Thousand.

EXPOSITION OF THE APOSTLES' CREED.

By Rev. J. DODDS, D.D., Corstorphine. 10th Thousand.

HISTORY OF THE ENGLISH BIBLE.

By Rev. GEORGE MILLIGAN, D.D., Caputh. 10th Thousand.

CHURCH, MINISTRY, AND SACRAMENTS.

By Rev. NORMAN MACLEOD, D.D., Inverness. 10th Thousand.

STUDIES IN THE ACTS OF THE APOSTLES.

By Rev. WM. ROBERTSON, M.A., Coltness. 10th Thousand.

LESSONS ON THE GOSPEL OF ST. MARK.

By Rev. A. I. ROBERTSON, D.D., Clackmannan. 10th Thousand.

THE APOSTLES' TEACHING.

PART I.—THE PAULINE THEOLOGY. By Rev. Professor PATERSON, D.D., University of Edinburgh. 10th Thousand.

EDINBURGH : GEO. A. MORTON, 42 GEORGE STREET.
R. & R. CLARK, LTD., 72 HANOVER STREET
(*Publication Agents to Church of Scotland*).

DATE DUE

GAYLORD			PRINTED IN U.S.A.